PIVOT A Vision for the New University

PIVOT

JOANNE
SOLIDAY

DR. MARK
LOMBARDI

A VISION
FOR THE
NEW
UNIVERSITY

CREDO
PRESS

Advantage.

Published by Advantage, Charleston, South Carolina.
Member of Advantage Media Group.

ADVANTAGE is a registered trademark, and the Advantage colophon is a trademark of Advantage Media Group, Inc.

Printed in the United States of America.

10 9 8 7 6 5 4 3 2

ISBN: 978-1-64225-056-5
LCCN: 2018964165

Cover design by Cisneros Design.
Emma L. Jones, Executive Editor, Credo Press.

This publication is designed to provide accurate and authoritative information in regard to the subject matter covered. It is sold with the understanding that the publisher is not engaged in rendering legal, accounting, or other professional services. If legal advice or other expert assistance is required, the services of a competent professional person should be sought.

Advantage Media Group is proud to be a part of the Tree Neutral® program. Tree Neutral offsets the number of trees consumed in the production and printing of this book by taking proactive steps such as planting trees in direct proportion to the number of trees used to print books. To learn more about Tree Neutral, please visit **www.treeneutral.com**.

Advantage Media Group is a publisher of business, self-improvement, and professional development books and online learning. We help entrepreneurs, business leaders, and professionals share their Stories, Passion, and Knowledge to help others Learn & Grow. Do you have a manuscript or book idea that you would like us to consider for publishing? Please visit **advantagefamily.com** or call **1.866.775.1696**.

For JRA ... always.
— *Mark Lombardi*

For Keith ... again, and again, and again.
— *Joanne Soliday*

Table of Contents

Endorsements

"At a time of true disruption in higher education, thought champions
with new strategic frameworks are needed to inspire change and
meaningful innovation. In this important work, Joanne Soliday
and Mark Lombardi position themselves accordingly, with a clear
codification of emerging challenges and opportunities facing
the independent sector and a roadmap for 'pivotal' institutional
leadership."
—Bob Bartlett, President, Michigan Colleges Alliance

"Soliday and Lombardi have given us a highly useful brief for
institutional change that covers both extreme disruption and
nuanced pivots. By examining case studies of successful leadership—
Mary Schmidt Campbell at Spelman, Dan Elsener at Marian, and
Amy Novak at Dakota Wesleyan—as well as Mark Lombardi at
Maryville, this volume will assist each president as he or she seeks
the appropriate position on a wide spectrum of approaches."
—Dr. Rich Ekman, President, Council of Independent Colleges

"Soliday and Lombardi provide a compelling call to action for today's college and university leaders. Your first pivot should be to read *Pivot: A Vision for the New University!*"
—*Barbara Lettiere, President, Immaculata University*

"College change may be yesterday's oxymoron, but it represents today's omni-mandate. Joanne Soliday and Mark Lombardi make a convincing argument, illustrated by multiple real-college cases, that cultivating institutional cultures adept at embracing and enacting strategic changes along five major fault lines with courage, speed, and agility—*pivoting*, that is—comprises the most essential change of all. This book is vital to understanding not only the *why* of pivotal change, but also the *what* and the *how*."
—*Dr. Ralph E. Enlow, Jr., President, Association of Biblical Higher Education*

"Written in a style accessible to all audiences and constituents, *Pivot: A Vision for the New University* promises to be the next must read for any member of a college or university community, particularly for those associated with an independent institution of higher learning. Soliday and Lombardi repeatedly prompt the reader about the urgent need to enact change, while reminding that the best call to action is one associated with positive institutional outcomes and improved student success."
—*Dr. Robert Wyatt, President, Coker College*

"Independent colleges and universities today face more challenges than ever. This book provides an essential framework for focusing mission and culture while transforming structure and approach. From classroom interaction to financial decision-making, Soliday and Lombardi offer creative advice for growing up into the twenty-first century."

—*Shirley Hoogstra, President, Council for Christian Colleges and Universities*

"Soliday and Lombardi know their stuff. The experiences they've had in higher education come shining through in their book, giving the reader an inside look at what many of the most innovative institutions of higher learning are doing to stay relevant. The authors talk about the importance of 'shifting the institutional culture from one of stasis to one of continuous innovation, change, and growth.' I can think of nothing more important than this when it comes to the creating a legacy for my presidency."

—*Jody Horner, President, Midland College*

Acknowledgments

Mark Lombardi

I cannot say enough about the outstanding work of Emma Jones on this project. Her editing skill, organization, insight, awesome experience, and good humor were instrumental in our working through the kinks and completing this project.

I want to thank Kathy Lunan and Jan Johnston who, behind the scenes, made so much of this book and all that Maryville has accomplished possible.

There are numerous faculty and staff at Maryville University who are innovative pioneers. They stretch themselves every day to constantly expand the boundaries of student learning. They are not stuck in the past and are courageous risk-takers. They are inspiring to me, and I am so proud of them.

I want to salute the best damn higher education leadership team anywhere in the United States. Those who are instrumental in all that we have accomplished both within and outside our learning spaces include Dr. Mary Ellen Finch, Dr. Jen McCluskey, Dr. Nina Caldwell, Dan Viele, Katherine Louthan, Cheri Fister, Shani Lenore, Jeff Miller,

Marci Sullivan, Dr. Mary Ellen Finch, Dr. Larry Hays, Dr. Stephanie Elfrink, Dr. Tammy Gocial, Dr. Steve Mandeville, Dr. Chuck Gulas, Margaret Onken, Jessica Norris, Mycah Faulkner, and Mario Morgan. Special mention goes to Dr. Jamie Washington for his great work on diversity and inclusion. I also need to profoundly thank Jerry Brisson and Fred Cisneros for their vision, creativity, and for always, always being there, no matter what.

And to my partner in this project and in so much over the years, Joanne Soliday—you are an inspiration for all who desire to make a difference in the lives of people. I love and respect you as a colleague, co-writer, advisor, and friend.

Joanne Soliday

Just months after I wrote my first book, *Surviving to Thriving: A Planning Framework for Leaders of Private Colleges and Universities*, in 2013, I started sticking notes of scribbled ideas to the newly printed pages, my mind spinning about the future. This book has allowed many of those thoughts to come to life, and I am grateful to those mentioned below for their support and engagement through this process.

The Credo team has been wonderful at continuing to share their experiences with me as they pull back the curtain on the inner workings of hundreds of colleges and universities across the country. A huge thank you to all of you for continuing to see value in my work and allowing me the best retirement transition that has ever been designed!

An additional word of special acknowledgement to Emma Jones for her continual support in making this book and so much possible at Credo. I will never be able to tell anyone else effectively what her skill, logic, and heart have meant to me in writing both of these books. I have told her that there would be no books without her, and

I mean it. She has an uncanny ability to hear my voice (and, in this book, to combine two voices!). I will never forget the experience of working with her and will watch her career with much excitement. My thanks also to Bill Fahrner for his incredible ability to manage a retiring partner with grace and accountability.

In my mind, the quality, success, and reputation of Credo have been crucial to my ability to write and have been driven by the relentless hard work and servant hearts of the Credo Executive Leadership Team. Tom Gavic, Bill Fahrner, Emma Jones, Dr. Joretta Nelson, and Tim Fuller have accumulated years of airline miles and hotel points because they believe in independent colleges from the depth of their souls! They have modeled a thirst for research, knowledge, and excellence that forms the foundation of Credo's solutions.

I wish I could mention every other member of the Credo team, but it would be impossible. Huge kudos to the project managers, researchers, and division leaders. They are at the core of the work we do, and they deliver it with quality and commitment. The home support team is crucial and so competent—from operations to marketing, I believe this team is the best. I will, however, lift up two others in this personal thank you. Susan Holt and Trudi Cary have been amazing partners to me in the logistical issues of writing this book and in the other meaningful work I continue to do. I turn to them for every small need and count on the way they receive my requests as important, while giving me encouragement at the same time.

Mark Lombardi has been a formidable partner in writing this book! His intense passion for innovation has inspired me. I will always be grateful to him for the confidence he has in me and the friendship we have forged.

Every day in this independent higher-education world, I find myself in awe of college presidents. Their ability to relentlessly search for solutions while wading through political land mines is admirable. It is through their eyes, and because of the endless hours they give, that I continue to be motivated to find and share best and next practices with them. My thanks to the faculty and staff at each institution across our country. They have been asked more and more to change how they do their work. I am grateful for their courage to take risks for the sake of the students they serve, and even more grateful for the ability to write a book that puts students at the center of learning and thinking in higher education.

My special thanks to the presidents, leadership teams, and boards of trustees at Dakota Wesleyan University, Marian University, Maryville University, and Spelman College. They were the perfect institutions to examine in the context of this book, because they have struggled and achieved with authenticity and transparency. They have put intensive effort toward embracing innovative and relevant cultures while continuing to change the lives of so many students along the way.

I am deeply motivated by my Christian faith and the local church that sustains me as I travel a road of deep faith in need of mentors, teachers, and companions along the way. Thank you to the pastors, elders, staff, and congregation of St. Mark's Church in Burlington, North Carolina.

It seems that I am always thanking my family for their tolerance of my insatiable desire to continue to make a difference. I know they thought I would stop at age seventy, but it didn't happen. Tambra, Ray, Jeremy, Cami, Vicki, Brian, Gavin, Christian, Julian, Lilly, Bev, John, Carole, Sherry, Janice, Jeff, Joyce, Bob, and my incredible mother-in-law, who still advises me at age 101 ... I am dependent upon your support and your love.

But most of all, much gratitude and love to my husband, Keith, who continues to lift up everything I do, every day.

Emma Jones

There were a number of critical participants in the development and evolution of this book to whom I owe debts of gratitude, and I am so pleased to be able to recognize them here. First and foremost, to Mark and Joanne: thank you for entrusting your words to me. It requires a particular vulnerability to bring forth ideas from a place of personal commitment and professional passion and have others examine them, pick them apart, and challenge them. Your willingness to allow me to do just that in the interest of creating the most powerful reflection of both your voices is recognized and appreciated. I am deeply honored to have served in this role with you. You are both courageous leaders to your core, and it is a gift to have had the opportunity to learn from you.

My Credo colleagues offered themselves up tirelessly as cheerleaders, brainstormers, problem-wrestlers, and co-editors; and for that, you all have my sincere thanks. Dr. Matt Trainum's examination of the landscape of research and knowledge around these pivot points was invaluable, as was his thoughtful editorial commentary. Dr. Joretta Nelson, Dr. Jennifer deCoste, and Michelle Samuels-Jones' expertise and insight enriched critical topics in the text and added important depth. My executive leadership team colleagues that Joanne has already mentioned stood in constant support of both me and this project. Tom, Joretta, Bill, and Tim—your confidence in me to bring this book to fruition was instrumental. My brand team members Sarah Cusick Kalajian, Catherine Rumley, and Anna Scott Pulliam leaned in to their roles and work on behalf of the firm with dedication and ownership, allowing me to place much-needed extra focus on this project.

Our external partners have been invaluable as well. Thanks to Jeff Spear of CFO Colleague and Dr. Steve Mandeville of Maryville University for sharing their expertise. From the first time I spoke with our external editor Mark Leichliter, I knew our partners at Advantage Media had matched us well. His ability to continually return to a focus on the reader's experience helped us take the chapters to the next level, and I am so appreciative of his precise, intellectual feedback. Similarly, Fred Cisneros, Paul Black, and Luli Chacon of Cisneros Design provided quick, excellent, thoughtful design that connected the concepts in the book to Credo's visual brand with great effectiveness.

I spent many, many days editing in the quiet, cozy confines of ShiftWork, my tiny community's co-working space. To all the Saxapahaw, North Carolina, friends and regulars who made those days feel not only creative, but connected to home, you have my thanks. Thank you finally to my wonderful family for their patience, love, and the amazing village they create.

Introduction

Mark Lombardi

I fell in love with the academy the first day I walked into an international relations class as a graduate teacher in 1982. Like most graduate instructors, we were thrown into the breach to teach introductory classes that tenured faculty were too busy or otherwise occupied with their research to teach. With no training save our love of the discipline, our ideals, and our desire to feed ourselves, we taught and taught and taught some more.

That was also the beginning of my subtle awareness that the academy had more than its fair share of incongruities. We were teaching thousands of students whose parents were paying large sums of money, but we were never trained to teach. Classes were structured solely around content, not student-learning theory. We assigned texts and crafted lectures that reflected our own undergraduate experience. The exams we gave usually tested only one method of learning. We graded them in the wee hours of the morning and then moved on to the next class. Those of us who fell in love with teaching and put a great deal of effort into it were labeled "non-researchers" by our faculty. Those who placed greater focus on research with their faculty mentors were deemed stars, destined for disciplinary greatness.

As a tenured faculty member at the University of Tampa, my love for the academy deepened. As with all great loves, though, familiarity exposed me to its underlying flaws, inconsistencies, and downright absurdities. I observed two deeply entrenched forces. The first was the academy's historic resistance to change. The second was self-preservation. An undercurrent of peer pressure told you at every turn that if you questioned the fundamental elements of the academy, the wrath of your colleagues would leave you ostracized at best and unemployed at worst. As I gradually turned to the "dark side" of education administration, the absurdities only grew, especially amidst the societal winds of change ushered in by the computer chip and all the transformations that have poured forth as a result.

Today, higher education is in the midst of a revolution as profound as the renaissance. It can and must reinvent itself around dynamic principles of mobility and flexibility, with student-centered engagement rooted in learning theory and data science. It must enter the twenty-first century, removing the shackles of stasis and cultural defense. Essentially, it must think and act in a wholly different manner.

> Today, higher education is in the midst of a revolution as profound as the renaissance.

The choice is clear. We can lead a revolution that makes higher education truly the centerpiece of an innovative and vibrant civil society, or we can defend our culture and methods and suffer what I fear will be a long and painful death. Universities around the country faced with this are stymied by a lack of courage, choosing inaction over urgency—with dire consequences for their ability to continue to serve their students well into the future.

This book is a call to my old first love. The revolution upon us is one that can revitalize the academy, making it central, relevant, and vibrant in service of all students. The tactics and strategies are right in front of us—all we have to do, as Lincoln said, is disenthrall ourselves of the quiet dogmas of the past. All we have to do is act.

Joanne Soliday

For most of my career, I have been intensely involved in helping colleges and universities take incremental steps toward health. The nine elements of the Thriving Framework®, explicated in my earlier book *Surviving to Thriving: A Planning Framework for Leaders of Private Colleges and Universities*, were all conceived because of their critical importance to the growth and sustainability of the colleges and universities I knew so well.

We know that action-oriented planning techniques are crucial, and that telling the story of an institution with distinction can make the difference in presenting the strength of its value proposition. Strong revenue streams, active and engaged learning, and campus spaces that encourage commitment and belonging are also markers of a thriving institution. The right use of data and modeling are central to everything above. And, in order to make it all happen, there is a compelling need for courageous leadership that results in culture change and greater levels of institutional self-esteem. I still believe it all! As I have contemplated what connects each of these elements to the future, I believe there is a new need to examine what thriving will mean as higher education changes.

It just isn't enough anymore for an institution to think about small, incremental growth steps to thriving. Every college is going to have to reexamine its ability to change direction in significant ways with courage, speed, and agility over the next ten years. As readers know well, the obstacles to change come in many forms. Sometimes the leadership team and board of trustees of the institution are not unified and healthy enough to inspire a culture of excitement and trust that will allow risk-taking. In other situations, the leadership team and the board might be ready to go, but the relationship between the faculty and administration needs deep repair. I, like you, could describe many specific situations representative of this challenge, but in the end, the ability to change is rooted in institutional culture. Everything Mark and I have written in this book will be dependent upon the shape of that culture. There simply isn't going to be a strategy that is strong enough to live in a culture of mistrust, apathy, or siloed thinking.

Over nearly twenty-five years in higher education consulting, questions about culture have arisen consistently in hundreds of my interactions. In exhaustive interviews and hundreds of strategy sessions, we almost always come around to culture as an obstacle to change. The conversations always begin with presidents asking about critical issues: How can issues in enrollment be solved? How can my advancement staff position me correctly to do the kind of fundraising necessary over the next years? What does student success really mean, and how can it be designed in a way to increase our retention rate and meet our mission? Of course, these are important and strategic questions. But quickly, we begin to see together that somewhere at the root of all these issues is the slow, subconscious flow of culture, informing the way we work and interact every day in ways we do not explicitly recognize, putting up barriers at so many turns to the strategies that will ultimately be critical to the future success of the institution and its students.

It is my hope that all of you reading this book will embrace the pivot points for which we advocate in these pages and will give careful thought to the multifaceted challenges and opportunities accompanying such change. These pivots require more, though, than shifts in operations or programs or business practices or even ways of leading—they require your commitment as institutional leaders to cultural change around accountability, agility, trust, appreciation, risk-taking, and individual learning and development. Maybe most of all, they require a spirit of self-awareness. You must be able to identify the gifts you can bring to bear—specific to your personal experience, leadership style, and character—on your own institutional culture in order to give wings to the implementation of pivotal change.

Toward the New University: Making the Pivot

The twenty-first century will become a Golden Age of learning. It will be an era where emerging technologies will create opportunities for all students to engage, experiment, hone their knowledge, and enhance their career skills. Students of any age will be empowered to learn according to their own pace and style. The university of the future—the *new university*—will lead this era as a center for innovation, where new ideas are continuously piloted, applied, and implemented; where higher education partners with businesses, school districts, and organizations to solve societal needs across a wide array of issues. It will be a space where the complex diversity of the American landscape will be seen, felt, and experienced such that all people will work within a culture of inclusion and appreciative engagement. We believe that the new university, where all this and much more is possible, is within our grasp. What we must do to make it a reality is to *pivot*.

Louis Soares of the American Council on Education said that the challenge to higher-education leaders is to "re-imagine their role from stewards of an existing enterprise to innovators of a new venture."[1] This book is for those who desire to face that challenge head-on. It is for presidents of colleges and universities who are willing to make a significant difference in the way we see learning and higher education in the twenty-first century, and for the board of trustee members who accept fiscal and missional responsibility for the long-term sustainability of those institutions. It is for faculty and staff whose daily interactions with learners inside and outside the classroom form the core of the student experience and whose work and dedication embody the missions our institutions serve. In short, it is for everyone who bears responsibility for bringing an institution of higher learning to its greatest level of effectiveness. We believe we all share the sacred trust of transforming lives that we have entered into with the students we have today and with the myriad of different learners we will meet in the years to come.

Defining a Pivot

As we explored our need to write this book, the concept of pivoting arose: a need to turn from some aspects of the culture of the institutions we had long known to the needs of the future. Once we began to say the word out loud to others, we heard many interpretations of what a pivot could mean in a college or university. A "pivot" is defined as a fixed point supporting something which turns or balances, or a person or thing on which something else depends. The powerful combination of these two definitions is

---

1   Louis Soares, "Post-traditional Learners and the Transformation of Postsecondary Education: A Manifesto for College Leaders," January 2013, https://www.acenet.edu/news-room/Documents/Post-Traditional-Learners.pdf.

exactly where we see institutions living out a pivot: finding the right points on which to change direction, with the success of the institution and its students depending upon that change.

A pivot does not look the same at all institutions. A pivot can be spurred by an external event; driven by a particular leader's vision for what an institution can become; unearthed by a grassroots shift in institutional culture and thinking; or come in response to student, community, or regional needs. Regardless of the origin or shape, the pivot drives action relentlessly. It requires a determined effort to ask the question *why* at all levels. Why do we do things this way? Why do we allow long-standing traditions of the academy to become obstacles to the opportunities that we now have for how we examine and approach learning? Pivoting means that we actually ask these questions and many more, explicitly, and then act to address them. It means not settling for a process or a curriculum or an experience that does not clearly have students at the center. It means turning all the way around to a new way of thinking and doing so with a spirit of risk and hope.

Pivoting also implies a new approach to change. We used to believe that an institution must focus first on operations, build to strategy, and then approach strategy with leverage in order to achieve significant change, but the urgency for change in so many institutions today often makes that linear and incremental approach irrelevant. We are now seeing more and more examples of institutions that approach strategy with leverage—with a pivot—and recreate the rest of the organization around it, with operations and mid-level strategy responding to the demands of the pivot. Pivoting gives us an opportunity to leapfrog over small, incremental steps, making the most important things happen.

Most common way

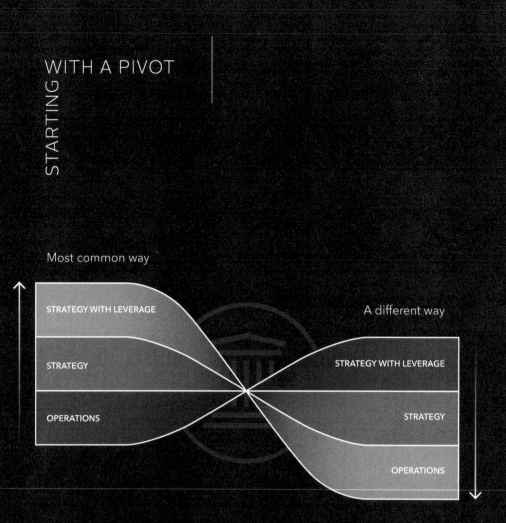

STRATEGY WITH LEVERAGE

STRATEGY

OPERATIONS

A different way

STRATEGY WITH LEVERAGE

STRATEGY

OPERATIONS

We are now seeing more and more examples of institutions
that start at strategy with leverage – with a pivot – and recreate
the rest of the organization around it, with operations and
mid-level strategy responding to the demands of the pivot.

We believe—and have seen in action—key areas around which pivots happen. We believe these pivot points offer the most significant opportunities for institutional transformation and carry the greatest urgency for needed change:

Courageous Leadership: Championing Disruption, Risk, and Innovation — With a richly shared vision between the president and the board, leaders across campus focused on change, and a reimagining of traditional structures of decision-making, the new university can shift the institutional culture from one of stasis to one of continuous innovation, change, and growth.

The Student at the Center: Transforming Learning for the Future — The rapid evolution of technology, the availability of vast quantities of data, ever-expanding research on how people learn and process differently, and the amount of information at every learner's fingertips begs critical questions about how we educate our students for a future we cannot yet fully comprehend; institutions must adapt and change accordingly.

No Margin, No Mission: Running a University in the Black — In order for us to be responsible to our missions and the students of the future, we must radically transform our approach to the business of our institutions, with intense focus on prioritizing strategy, centralizing decision-making, building partnerships, and realigning budgetary processes with difference-making initiatives.

The Explosion of Adult Education: Meetings Society's Needs — As technology and artificial intelligence transform the workplace, and thirty to forty million workers across the United States will require continuous education to remain gainfully employed, institutions of higher learning face a critical imperative to invest in all types of learners, elevating individuals, families, and communities in the process.

Opportunity and Inclusion: Diversifying the Campus Culture

— The backgrounds of students entering higher education is changing rapidly, becoming more and more diverse across lines of race, ethnicity, religion, ability and disability, socioeconomic status, gender expression, and sexual orientation; colleges and universities must acknowledge that these diverse groups have been historically limited in their access to higher education and/or not appropriately supported and served once on campus, and place intentional focus on creating inclusive campus communities to meet the needs of these diverse learners.

The New University: Institutional Stories

Throughout the book, we will talk about the "new university." What we envision is in some respects a kind of learning utopia: physical and virtual spaces of higher learning reimagined with student learning, access, innovation, relevance, and sustainability at their very core. We envision that the new university will educate students of all ages, and that they will be at the center of learning and teaching. The ability to guide students toward a fulfilling life with the skills they need to be successful in the workplace and the values they need to be citizens of the world will be at the center of this utopia. It may be that no one institution can achieve this vision in totality, but we believe all institutions should undertake their own blue-sky reimagining and pivot toward it. The colleges and universities we introduce below have pivoted in this way—powerfully, with intention, and with measurable results.

Our interactions with the presidents of the four institutions introduced here, and other courageous leaders like them, have been central to our thinking. Their journeys have not been without challenges and failures, but these presidents did not settle for incremental change. They looked carefully at what was ahead and pivoted. Watching these presidents and their teams lead strategically, all in ways unique to their style and institutional missions, renewed our hope that all colleges and universities have an opportunity to be more innovative than they have ever been. The presidents you will meet in these pages would also tell you that they are nowhere near finished. When change and innovation become inherent in the culture, progress is continuous and ongoing. Central to these stories is a shift in institutional culture that leaders so often wish for. Each of these institutions recognizes that innovation and change are not smooth or simple paths to follow, because, in so many cases, there is no precedent—they are the trailblazers. Yet all of these leaders believe that it is worth the risk to keep trying, to break the mold, and to continually recommit to new ways of serving their students. In the end, it all comes back to courageous leadership. Courage lives at the heart of innovation, risk, and change, and our leaders will have to take the leap of faith that courage demands.

Dakota Wesleyan University, Mitchell, South Dakota: Collaboration and Entrepreneurship for Relevance in Learning

Dr. Amy Novak, president of Dakota Wesleyan University (DWU), has made it possible for us to tell every institution that location should not be an inhibitor, that innovation grounded in students and the local economy can create monumental success. Innovation gave a small university in South Dakota the ability to leapfrog over its peers. With a commitment to make DWU an active leader, collaborative partner, and incubator for economic growth and entrepreneurial thinking in South Dakota[2], President Novak has focused energy and resources around developing innovative partnerships with technical colleges, industries, and businesses most important to the state's economic health. As a result, DWU is leading efforts in rural workforce development in the critical areas of health care and education. DWU has placed a laser focus on relevance in the core curriculum, in part through using a business advisory group representative of significant local industry sectors to examine how best to equip students for the future. The resulting energy and momentum on campus has transformed institutional self-esteem, with skyrocketing levels of engagement by board members, faculty, staff, and students.

Before its pivot, like so many small colleges in rural communities, DWU was in slow decline. In 2007, a senior faculty member summarized the institutional self-esteem of DWU in the following manner: "DWU is a mediocre university, with a mediocre faculty, mediocre facilities, in a mediocre community." At the conclusion of a visit from the Higher Learning Commission at the time, the commission described the faculty relationship with the then-president as "highly tenuous," and the university without focus. The institution's enrollment hovered between 550 and 600, and accounts receivable exceeded $1.2 million. Budgets consistently in the red characterized the previous decade. Retention rates from freshman to junior year lingered around 55 percent. Disagreements between church leaders and board members had created a culture of

---

2   "Inclusive and Intentional," Dakota Wesleyan University, accessed October 12, 2018, https://www.dwu.edu/about-dwu/mission-values.

distrust within the board and across the university. Administrators continually apologized for what it did not have or could not deliver.

Confronted by a glaring budget shortfall and the loss of strong faculty, the university faced a critical decision: courageously reposition itself or continue its struggle for survival with an almost certain end. Under the leadership of a new financial officer and with Dr. Novak newly seated as provost, in collaboration with the president and key board of trustee leadership, the university hired an outside firm to conduct an extensive market analysis of its competitive strengths and weaknesses. The results of this analysis led the leadership team to embark on a bold new strategy to reposition the university. Ever since, there has been a fierce determination in this campus community to be relevant and of service to their community, region, and state. In their efforts to turn their focus to the region, they have tackled change with a rare sense of urgency and rich culture of accountability. One of the greatest lessons we can learn from DWU is that you don't have to understand exactly how an initiative will finish in order to bring energy to the start. So often we are tempted to believe that it takes "big" efforts to be successful; instead, what we know about DWU is that it was an aggregation of changes, with clear vision at the center, that built toward a powerful institutional shift.

The first, and possibly most critical, change for the institution was that DWU stopped apologizing for who it was. Owning, celebrating, and communicating their identity drove institutional self-esteem up across campus and began to change the culture. Strategic initiatives took on a whole new level of energy as institutional self-esteem increased. This university is a perfect example of how momentum and excitement surges in a positive atmosphere. Organizational culture matters at DWU—the institution identified faculty who believed in the mission and the strategic initiatives that supported it, investing in faculty success while honoring the culture and ethos of the region.

With a fiercely individualistic ethos and a deeply engrained entrepreneurial spirit, South Dakota presented a unique opportunity for the institution to build energy around the development of innovative partnerships that connected it to regional businesses and employment pipelines, for the benefit of both DWU students and the surrounding communities. They went from being a university *in* the community to becoming a university *of and for* the community by inviting business and industry to become partners in creating a rural renaissance that celebrated the local spirit of innovation and opportunity. Rural regions ought not to be viewed through a stereotypical lens of stagnation. Instead, they deserve leadership from universities prepared to thoughtfully engage in entrepreneurial partnerships that strengthen economic opportunities, leverage technology, and demonstrate a commitment to innovation and entrepreneurial activity within a context of limited resources. In other words, rural regions require universities equipped to demonstrate engagement and responsiveness to emerging needs. Small colleges can significantly impact a region when they demonstrate models of innovative engagement among the university, the communities it serves, the region it supports, and the countless partners who collectively seek to strengthen the place in which they have invested their future.

The university now operates with a partnership mind-set, propelled by a mission to fuel its region with entrepreneurial leadership equipped to bring sustainable growth to the Great Plains. In addition to driving institutional self-esteem, this has enabled the university to secure significant philanthropic and collaborative resources and has ignited enrollment. The results are astounding:

- Today, nearly 100 percent of the faculty and staff give to the university annual fund, compared to less than 50 percent a decade ago.

- In the last five years, the university has secured more than $40 million in gifts to strengthen access through scholarships and expand and improve facilities. These include a new center for the study of health care, fitness, and sciences; a new state-of-the-art athletic and wellness facility; and a new theater and welcome center. Plans are in progress to start construction on a new School of Business Innovation and Leadership in the fall of 2019.

- Student accounts receivable are now under $150,000.

- For the last nine years, the university has run a budget in the black. New, targeted online programs designed to meet regional labor-force demands have grown by more than 250 percent in three years, meeting both the institution's mission and need for increasing and diversified revenue streams.

- DWU has seen ten years of record growth in enrollment.[3]

DWU now stands as one of the most compelling models for small, rural colleges to watch. As we publish this book (2018), the leadership of the college is on the cusp of piloting more initiatives to deepen their commitment to South Dakota, its rural communities,

---

3   Statistics shared by official Dakota Wesleyan University sources. Additional institutional statistics on each college and university can be found in Appendix I.

and the students at the center of this relevant and responsive education.

Marian University, Indianapolis, Indiana:
Distinction Through Programmatic Innovation and Growth

With a background in Catholic K–12 education and foundation work, Daniel J. Elsener, president of Marian University of Indianapolis, did not set out to become a college president. And yet, he has become a leader for innovation in Catholic higher education. The opening of a college of osteopathic medicine at Marian, only the second medical school in the state of Indiana, propelled the university into visibility and pushed other facets of the institution toward excellence in new ways. The medical college was the result of asking the right questions: What does the city of Indianapolis need, and how can we meet that need in a way consistent with our mission? Thus began Marian's pivot—searching out and asking the right questions in every scenario to push for new, relevant solutions. This type of thinking became a thread through the development of new curricular and co-curricular programs. The focus on strong financial and academic models around high-quality medical teaching led to similar examinations in business and education. As visibility and excitement rose, so did a new success in philanthropy and grant funding. Marian is on the move, with inspiring levels of enthusiasm and motivation across campus toward the success of their students, their city, and their region.

President Elsener talks about the beginning of his time at Marian University, then Marian College, in 2001 with a humble spirit. The indicators of Marian's problems were multifaceted and obvious. Chipped paint, broken sidewalks, and potholes spoke to high levels of deferred maintenance. Enrollment and fundraising declines plagued the institution, and Marian was running significant operational deficits, which were tipping toward banking-support issues. During his interviews for the presidency, President Elsener heard an almost desperate need for a strategic direction that would achieve the results necessary for Marian's sustainability. Once he assumed the role, one day in July of that year stands out as the clearest example of the gravity of the situation.

President Elsener said, "I arrived at work very early in the morning as usual, happy and rested after a three-day Fourth of July celebration. The first person in my office that morning was the vice president for enrollment. He informed me our freshman class would fall significantly short of enrollment projections." With a smaller-than-expected class, retention problems, and limited part-time students, total enrollment would be just over one thousand students. This was not going to provide the revenue they needed to be a viable institution.

"Next, I had a surprise visit from fundraising leadership. They informed me that we would be short of the cash and pledge goals that we needed so much to meet our deficit. After the fundraising news came our beloved and straightforward chief financial officer, who had arrived on the scene a few months before I did. He informed me that we only had $70,000 available for capital improvements, which was barely enough to buy the paint and fix the broken desks and tables that dotted various classrooms across campus. It was certainly not enough to fix the larger problems that we had. I remember distinctly looking up at the clock when the CFO left my office; it wasn't even nine thirty in the morning, and a trilogy of very bleak news had been laid on my shoulders. Clearly, it was this morning when the real fireworks went off and it hit me: Marian's very survival was in serious question."

President Elsener says that he was reminded of a phrase at that moment: it's always darkest before the dawn. It was the moment that he said to himself, "Let's get ready for the dawn, and a major and mighty revival of Marian." In the summer of his first year, Marian's leadership team came together to discuss the essence of Marian's mission and how that translated to the campus community. They reaffirmed their core values of responsible stewardship, dignity of the individual, reconciliation, and peace and justice. They embraced four clear goals:

1. to more fully live out their core Catholic and Franciscan values;

2. to advance academic quality;

3. to make the campus a more vibrant and life-giving community in which to study, learn, and grow; and,

4. to make sure there were enough resources to attain the first three goals exceptionally.

Over the course of the following years, with the deep commitment of the college's leadership, financial and missional support from The Sisters of St. Francis, and steadfast belief from the Marian community, the institution improved its foundational standing financially and operationally. Initial momentum behind its transformation came from an unexpected source: the addition of football to its athletics roster. The start-up of the football program and its quick success was the first time in a long time that many began to believe things could change, that Marian could plan to do something substantial and execute that plan. The football program brought increased enrollment and revenue but also a new spirit of pride for the campus and the surrounding community. It opened the door for the design of strategic, intentional enrollment pipelines, both curricular and co-curricular, that continue to increase the revenue influx into the university.

As the college became stronger, its opportunity for transformation grew. The president and chief operating officer of Eli Lilly and Company at the time, Dr. John C. Lechleiter, and his wife Sarah were working with Marian on a campaign to expand the university. Dr. Lechleiter pointed out to Marian's leadership that most great cities in America have a great Catholic university and believed that Marian could become that for Indianapolis. This idea sparked a new wave of excitement within Marian's leadership, and a new vision formed around that goal. With extraordinary levels of hope, risk, and alignment to vision, an institutional pivot began that would result in the 2009 announcement that Marian College was to become Marian University, with a continued commitment to the Franciscan value of meeting critical needs in the world. The growth since that time has been significant:

- Marian's Make History campaign, which launched in 2007, blew past a campaign consultant's estimate of $35 million, past Marian's aggressive campaign goal of $68 million, and concluded with a total of $163 million in donations by the end of 2012. "While an institution of our size and diversity garnering $163 million will receive much national attention," President Elsener said at the time, "what will forever impress and edify me is the profound transformation of our institution and what this transformation will enable us to do to better serve our students in Indianapolis, Indiana, the nation, and beyond."[4]

---

4   Bob Golobish, "Marian University's $163 Million Campaign Makes History," February 2013, https://www.marian.edu/newsroom/newsitem/2013/02/05/ marian-university's-$163-million-campaign-makes-history.

- 80 percent FTFT retention (up from 59 percent in 2001)

- $129.1 million in net assets (up from $8.9 million in 2001)

- $111.1 million annual revenue (up from $14.1 million in 2001)

- $2 million per month average in fundraising (up from $1.5 million for the year in 2001)

- Just over $40 million in new construction completed between 2016 and 2018

- Four thousand+ total students in 2018–19 academic year (up from eleven hundred students in 2001)

- 1,126 graduate students (up from twelve in 2001), with more than six hundred in the college of osteopathic medicine

- Fourth-fastest growing Catholic baccalaureate college in the country.[5]

Maryville University, St. Louis, Missouri: Creating the Active Learning Ecosystem

A note from Joanne:

It is because of the extraordinary pivots at Maryville University that I first asked Mark if he would be willing to think about writing a book with me. He has been and is a determined student of the future in higher education and learning. Walking beside Maryville in a partnership spanning more than fifteen years, I have had the extraordinary privilege to be able to watch the transformation myself as the institution embarked on a distinctive journey to create and execute a new direction.

---

5 Statistics shared by official Marian University sources. Additional institutional statistics on each college and university can be found in Appendix I.

As the new president at Maryville in 2007, Dr. Mark Lombardi was adamant that existing methods of teaching and learning and the higher education structures and systems that support them would not be sufficient for the future. Centered around the creation of their Active Learning Ecosystem (A.L.E.), the leadership has pushed at the edges of every preconceived idea of how a university operates. Before any new initiative is brought to the table, Maryville administration, staff, and faculty have to be able to answer the question, "How will this benefit students?" The pride that comes from making a significant impact on student learning has been a critical momentum-builder that drives continuous change and action across the institution. Unwavering attention to institutional effectiveness and student outcomes, couched in a future-focused approach to learning design, risk-taking, and innovation in every area has catapulted Maryville to its status as an increasingly recognized regional and national institution.

A decade ago, Maryville was a 140-year-old private university serving the St. Louis area, the states of Missouri and Illinois, and the Midwest. It is fair to say that Maryville University was not well known in higher-education circles. Between 2007–2014, Maryville expanded its recruitment reach to Texas and the West Coast, brought in an expanded international student population (growing from eight in 2007 to 250 in 2014), and generated annual surpluses averaging 5 to 7 million dollars per year. In 2015, a new strategic plan at Maryville was designed and initiated, and with it came an aggressive mandate to revolutionize learning inside and outside the classroom and expand access and opportunity for students from across the United States while increasing effectiveness and student-learning outcomes. Based on that mandate, President Lombardi cast a vision for the campus community and set the stage for Maryville to become a central and compelling player in a learning ecosystem that would change the face of higher education. As a result, the pace of disruptive change is intense and continuous, requiring high levels of resiliency and performance across campus. He shared the following assumptions during convocation in 2015:

- Content does not belong to professors only. Content has become democratized at a feverish pace through the digitization of knowledge.

- Learning theory, brain research, and youth development has shown us that standardized testing and other "objective" measures are not, and should not be, predictors of either access, ability, or ultimate success.

- Higher education costs have outstripped people's ability to pay, which means education has become a commodity subject to all the forces of the marketplace.

- Time spent sitting in a classroom has little or no relationship to mastery of a subject, or the ability to apply that knowledge in a real-world setting.

- Education *is* the answer, but we must change and adapt or face irrelevancy.

With these assumptions at the core, President Lombardi put forth a set of principles that would guide Maryville's strategic trajectory:

- Students are at the center of the classroom, of learning, and of outcomes.

- All learners have their own style, pace, and approach to learning. Pedagogy must be as flexible as the learner.

- Problem-solving, digital literacies, collaboration, and outcomes must be the focus in teaching.

- Mobility and flexibility are the new normal.

- The entire campus, inside and outside, should be a vibrant learning space.

Convocation speeches like this one each year have provided a touchstone for the campus community around the momentum at Maryville. But inspiring speeches are not what makes success happen—change has been accomplished because of the integrated effort of the board of trustees, administration, faculty, and staff all moving in the same direction with clear expectation and purpose, with extraordinary results:

- 88 percent FTFT retention

- 97 percent job placement rate

- Third fastest-growing private university in the nation

- Five nationally ranked programs in nursing, cybersecurity, sports-business management, interior design, and actuarial science

- Named an Apple Distinguished School for 2016–2018; recognized for its Digital World program, which gives students the opportunity to personalize their education in an enhanced technology environment

- Ranked in the top 10 percent of all major universities in the nation for the economic value of its academic degrees by Educate to Career, a non-profit firm that analyzes the value of a college degree in response to student demand for good return on investment (ROI)

- Consistently ranked by *Forbes* and Kiplinger's Personal Finance magazine as a top private school; named by Kiplinger's to its list of one hundred best values in private colleges and universities for seven consecutive years; named by *Forbes* on its "Best Colleges" list for the past three years.[6]

When you ask leadership team members at Maryville what the next pivot conversation will be, they are unified around a concern about access and pricing. They understand that as they become more and more popular and growth continues, there are many questions to answer about how they continue to be affordable and accept the students they have always loved and respected. At this time, Maryville has no plans to become more selective. The plan instead is to become better and better at meeting students where they are and taking them to their highest potential in an individualized way.

Maryville intends to expand its mission dramatically by increasing the number of adult students it will reach. There is a philosophy of lifelong learning at Maryville that embraces innovation and the experience of those who are seeking more education. The increase in adult students will be crucial, because it aligns mission with market need so beautifully, but Maryville also sees this work as direct service to the community. The university has been front and center as a partner to the city in a variety of ways, and with this new initiative to be on the cutting edge of learning directed at the adult workforce, the partnership deepens.

One thought expressed by all of the leaders at Maryville University is that they are not afraid to fail. From the most senior board member to those on the front lines, everyone is clear that

---

6   Statistics shared by official Maryville University sources.

innovation demands risk, and everyone is clear that innovation will be rewarded. The stage is set at Maryville to explore the future and embrace any initiative that can contribute to personalized student learning and ultimately to student success.

Spelman College, Atlanta, Georgia:
Excellence in Women's Education with Boldness and Confidence

Spelman College has been the premier leader in higher education for Black women in the United States for many years, taking extraordinary pride in bringing into crisp focus women's ability to make change in the world. With Dr. Mary Schmidt Campbell as president, the college has grown into its boldness, moving an already thriving institution to even higher levels of success. Spelman is home to a lived culture of empowering a historically marginalized group of learners, currently leading the nation in the number of Black women who graduate in STEM areas. Critical metrics across constituent engagement, from alumni giving to student retention (especially in the area of STEM), are on the rise. By effectively connecting vocation, confidence, emotional IQ, academic hope, and personalized learning, Spelman is able to confidently nurture each student along her journey.

Although women of African descent, historically and into the present, have been regarded by some as one of the most oppressed, marginalized, and disenfranchised groups, Spelman does not see their students in that way. Quite the contrary: at Spelman, Black women are center stage, regarded as precious assets, offering invaluable gifts and talents to be honed and perfected. The Spelman experience embraces and leverages the strength of its cultural heritage as a framework for why and how their students will achieve. At Spelman, advancing women of color is not what they do, it is who they are. The pivot at Spelman is to outperform and achieve at unprecedented levels. While they have achieved extraordinary excellence among Historically Black Colleges and Universities (HBCU) and remain deeply connected to that identity, it is not the only standard by which they wish to be judged. Spelman is unequivocal about its vision to be one of the nation's most significant liberal arts colleges, with no apologies for being a women's college. If you ask those who live and work there, this is a highly achievable task. They know the women they teach, they focus on the way they learn, and they know that they want them to succeed in the world by making an extraordinary difference.

To understand the influence of Spelman, one must look beyond the walls of Spelman, beyond the city of Atlanta, beyond US borders, and to the world. Spelman produces Black women who thrive, in a world which is often not created for, or inclusive of, Black women. Spelman is forcing American higher education and industries to create space for women leaders of African descent, leading systemic change with determination and clarity of focus.

President Campbell believes that Spelman has to be the place that permits its students to study their identity and blossom into it. Across the institution, every faculty and staff member is dedicated to the transformation of Black women through learning and increased self-esteem. Their ability to personalize each woman's experience and give her the confidence to change something in the world has been central to the levels at which their students perform, complete, and succeed post-college. The absolute conviction that graduates of this small college in Atlanta could have an impact on the world remains a driving force for change at an institution already grounded in a strong foundation of mission, propelling the institution forward in powerful ways:

- Two-thirds of graduates go on to obtain advanced degrees

- Recognized as one of the leading producers of Fulbright Fellowship winners

- Recognized by the National Science Foundation as the leading producer of Black women who go on to earn doctorate degrees in the sciences

- Ranked number one HBCU by the U.S. News & World Report

- Ranked number two in Best Value Schools - Best Historically Black Colleges and Institutions

- Ranked number three for Students' Top Schools for Inspiration by the *Wall Street Journal/New York Times* Higher Education Survey

- Listed among Peace Corps' 2016 top volunteer-producing Historically Black Colleges and Universities[7]

Many institutions are positioning themselves to pivot. You might be reading this book and determining where you stand. It is our great hope that you will be a part of this revolution in higher education. We wish to instigate a movement that will begin by asking the question "why" every time you plan or undertake a new initiative. A movement that will demand open minds as we begin to educate a whole new generation of students who have the ability to access infinite information on demand and are hungry for those who might facilitate their understanding and help them apply what they've learned to the vocations they will choose. A movement that

---

7   Statistics shared by official Spelman College sources. Additional institutional statistics on each college and university can be found in Appendix I.

will embrace learning for people of every age and provide exactly what they need to do their own significant work.

We have been intentionally provocative and assertive in our vision for what could be. The philosophies and strategies examined have been embraced in various ways by the institutions featured throughout to help us all see what is possible. It is true that the universities we have chosen to discuss will not know the results of their efforts for years to come. We can tell you why they decided to pivot, and we can tell you how, but part of the story is that there will be no progress toward innovation in higher education without risk. It takes courage to pivot, and it's our hope that seeing it in action will spark leaders with courage to act.

Courageous Leadership: Championing Disruption, Risk, and Innovation

The strongest college and university presidents possess extraordinary levels of creativity, courage, and passion. They have the ability to raise capital, manage a complex financial organization, communicate effectively with varied constituent groups, and engage and partner with the corporate community. They are hired with a mandate to grow and sustain an institution consistent with its mission.

But the culture those presidents enter is frequently resistant to change, challenges institutional innovation except in the most incremental of terms, and values decision-making by consensus more highly than rapid action. Pockets of deeply entrenched power throughout the institution limit or entirely disable the ability to explore change and take risks. Boards of trustees are often not positioned to support leadership effectively through change and are not educated around the need for innovative thought and action. We see this play out over and over again as leaders watch the tension grow on campuses around the country between those who recognize the imperative for change and those mired in stasis. The struggle to move the culture of the institution to a place of agility and courageous decision-making is frequently one of the greatest challenges that college and university leaders face. Their ability to do so can determine the success or failure of their presidency, as well as that of the institution they lead.

The fundamental predicate for a culture of risk-taking and innovation is that experimentation is essential to discovering better ways of doing things with speed and flexibility, especially in this world of rapid change and adaptation. The obvious beneficiaries of an innovative culture are our students, and ultimately, their learning and success. In such a culture, failure is lauded as a learning exercise on the path to success, and a key assumption is that the way we do things now can always be made better.

Higher education has existed largely in its current form for over one hundred and thirty years. Depending on how you trace the creation of the modern university, the current institutional structure and organization is remarkably similar to those institutions which evolved and developed from the 1870s through the early twentieth century. Departments and disciplines have come and gone, graduation requirements have changed, and the growth of accrediting bodies has reshaped university academic and non-academic business to some extent, but the overall structure remains, and is deeply entrenched at most universities and colleges throughout the western world. As you have recognized in the institutions you inherited, the authority for governing universities has evolved over the decades into spheres of influence, where primary authority for some decisions rest with administration, others with faculty, and other decisions are jointly owned. While this concept of shared governance has different manifestations at different universities depending upon their history and philosophy, it has created a culture that has discouraged experimentation and action in favor of slow, deliberative analysis. Courage, risk-taking, and innovation have not been supported or rewarded. Innovators at all levels of a university are typically viewed negatively as disrupters, tamped down precisely because they challenge established norms regarding services, information, pedagogy, or definitions of student success. As we experience with regularity, the academic culture is one marked by incrementalism, fear of change, and the valuing of consensus and agreement over action and initiative.

Resistance to change had not been significantly challenged in higher education until the explosion of the digital age. The movement into a digitized information age has altered the very foundation of education, and many colleges and universities have been slow to realize it. As the corporate sector found itself in a constant state of adaptation in order to reflect rapid market disruption, higher education remained largely separate from such patterns. Once isolated in a state of stasis, higher education now experiences the realities of the marketplace within its walls. The demands of a rapidly evolving digital world, the democratization of knowledge, the availability and access of content, and the fierce market demands of demographic change combined with price sensitivity and public scrutiny of higher education have illuminated and amplified the academy's shortcomings. As a vital sector of the society, those shortcomings are now exposed.

Since 2000, and particularly since the great recession of 2008, analysts have warned about the number of colleges and universities that may close their doors.[8] As discount rates and broken financial models plague higher education, the industry has been focused on the ability of institutions to merely weather the financial storm rather than change a broken model. Though the financial issues are still in front of us, the challenges are clear: How can colleges and universities reframe growth and sustainability in radically transformative ways? How do we think and act differently in order to deliver the most relevant, affordable learning opportunities to the most diverse student body the world has ever seen? How do we develop the courage to flip our campus culture of stagnation to one of innovation?

> How can colleges and universities reframe growth and sustainability in radically transformative ways?

What has become clear, and what continues to be absolutely essential to flipping that culture, is the extraordinary need for courageous leadership. Courageous leadership is required to question old assumptions, mobilize needed resources, focus strategic energy, and articulate a clear vision. More than ever, we recognize that strong leaders question and disrupt the status quo in order to remain relevant and meet the needs of learners into the future. In higher education institutions that are driving change, courageous leaders put a laser focus on:

1. Rallying the board of trustees around a strong vision for the future of the institution while re-organizing its members to be champions of innovation.

---

8   Kelly Woodhouse, "Closures to Triple," Inside Higher Ed, September 28, 2015, https://www.insidehighered.com/news/2015/09/28/moodys-predicts-college-closures-triple-2017.

2.   Relentlessly searching for and developing change and innovation leadership across the institution in order to shift culture.

3.   Breaking down the barriers to innovation and risk-taking within the culture and organization of the faculty.

4.   Abandoning the notion of consensus in favor of adaptation; action; and a vibrant, strategic committee structure for the institution and the board.

1. Creating a Shared Vision: The President and the Board

Presidents discuss a central tension with their peers: How involved should they get with their boards? But this is fundamentally the wrong question: the real question is not the board's degree of involvement, but rather how presidents focus their involvement on the vision and the subsequent strategies to achieve it. The new university is one where the president and the board of trustees spend their time together with a strategic focus on vision: communicating, connecting, and building where the university is going, how fast it needs to move, and how it will get there. Once the board buys into the vision, then the discussion of macro-strategy has a context and a framework of understanding. Without that, the board is simply reacting to a series of seemingly unrelated decisions, and that is where misunderstanding and opposition can emerge. Keeping the board at arm's length means they do not have true or rich context for the change that is essential. Leaders need to be able to function knowing that their boards have their backs even through difficult and unfamiliar territory. Courageous presidents cannot be effective change agents with constant worry about no-confidence votes and board intervention in management issues. In short, just when they think they are spending too much time with their board on vision, they should spend a little bit more.

It was the commitment of the board of trustees that jump-started Maryville University's journey. This engaged and passionate board has created space and safety for change that has been crucial in the university's ability to pivot. Fundamentally, the Maryville board has made a comprehensive philosophical and strategic commitment to a new approach to education. The institutional vision demands their engagement. Vice Chair of the board Jim Switzer says, "I have been a part of many great things in my life, but I don't think I have ever been prouder of anything than what we have done for student learning at Maryville University." Giving legs to a bold vision will always begin with crafting the right board of trustees for the work that must be done. At Maryville, board members were selected specifically because of skills or experiences that bear a connection to innovative work, and these connections are explicit to their appointment and engagement. They know their role, have clear expectations, and serve as active contributors to institutional momentum without the micromanagement that slows many administrations down.

Maryville board members felt that their institutional heritage, through its founding within the Sacred Heart tradition, had a strong connection to academic innovation and student success, as articulated in the institutional history: "This heritage bequeathed to us by the Religious of the Sacred Heart includes a commitment to the education of the whole person through programs designed to meet the needs of traditional and non-traditional students offered in day, evening, weekend and blended formats. We are committed to provide an excellent, challenging, mentoring education where students are free to explore issues of ethics, spiritual place, and questions of conscience." While Maryville has been a secular institution since 1973, the fact that the sisters at Maryville embedded a long-valued culture around individual success for all students fueled a new conversation about what student success could look like today and in the future.

The relationship to institutional foundation here is critical: too often, innovation and traditional values seem destined to come into conflict with each other. It was clear that the Maryville board of trustees had embraced the best of both. Believing that a liberal arts education was still instrumental in the success of its students, the university embraced that core and surrounded it with a new and innovative model for education.

In every university, the task of the board of trustees is twofold: they have ultimate fiduciary responsibility over the university, and they hire and fire the president or chancellor. The best boards are mindful of these two direct roles and exercise engagement with both while also giving the president the room and freedom to manage the university in all other arenas. In this sense, effective boards must be both invested in the strategic direction of the university and also trustful of the president and the myriad tactical management decisions he or she must make to move the institution forward. Without a mutual understanding of vision at the proverbial thirty thousand foot level, the board can't possibly understand the complexity of the decisions demanded of presidents. Since there is never a straight line from innovation, to achievement, and ultimately to success, the board must have the kind of relationship with the president where they understand the ebbs and flows of decision-making. Navigating the politics of change within the academy rests on the most crucial element of board-president relations when it comes to vision: they must have a clear awareness that together they

/ing the university from a culture of stasis and resistance
ge to one of innovation, risk-taking, and change celebration
designed to achieve one singular and unwavering outcome: the
facilitation and maximization of student learning.

Together, the president and the board of trustees are changing the university from largely a culture of stasis and resistance to change to one of innovation, risk taking, and change celebration.

Moreover, embracing the vision is central to understanding the accelerated pace at which decisions must be made. The traditionally glacial movement of colleges and universities must be jettisoned for a much more market-driven, responsive, action-oriented approach. Institutional vision in the twenty-first century academy must build upon speed, flexibility, and responsiveness, requiring that the board and the president understand not only what the vision is, but the ways in which it can be decisively and quickly realized through strong planning and bold initiatives. One of the best examples we've seen of how vision can drive strategic action at the board level is at institutions where the board of trustees' committee structure is reorganized directly around advisory groups connected to the themes in the strategic plan. When that happens, board members have a focus that has a direct impact on the health of the college or university and the life of the students. It brings critical relevance to every board discussion. Many college presidents and board chairs are afraid to restructure, because there are long-standing traditions and constructs. But with the vision at the center of the board's connection to the president, it is irresponsible to allow those entitlements to block the excitement and innovation of the future.

The reorganization of the board around DWU's strategic plan has been critical to the success of that institution's vision. In doing so, board members have been reenergized around the mission and empowered to be active players in the institution's growth and success. They are now deeply engaged in work around themes of strategic growth, visibility, the learning experience, innovative partnerships, and a sustainable foundation.[9] They are leaning in—with their time, energy, and resources—to the development of DWU's Center for Rural Impact, which will become an applied-research laboratory for four cornerstones of the rural renaissance: economic development, health care, ministry/non-profit administration, and education. Additionally, regional leaders, along with university faculty, are collaborating on the interface of digital pedagogy and experiential learning, rethinking how to deliver health care, support rural education, and strengthen rural communities. President Novak has been intentional about providing education and training that has given this board a sense of urgency and compelled them to stand behind an agile system for change. Not only do they embrace and read everything that is delivered to them, but they are now sending reading materials to President Novak as well.

Spelman College offers us another example of a strong orientation toward action rooted in the strategic plan. The board of trustees at Spelman is as prestigious and talented as the women who study and graduate there. Over these last ten years, the leadership of the board has pushed the institution to function at more strategic levels. That is easier done when the budget is balanced, and growth is happening at all levels, and the board has taken advantage of Spelman's positive position to aggressively educate themselves about

---

9   "Our Institutional Strategic Plan, 2014 – 2020," Dakota Wesleyan University, September 2018, https://www.dwu.edu/about-dwu/dwu-strategic-plan.

the future of higher education. Generally, institutional culture either propels growth, innovation, and success, or impedes it. Spelman College is a model of the former. As such, they are proud of who they are, proud of each other individually, and focus on their collective successes. Though success can sometimes breed complacency, this college and its board have focused on being aware of its current strengths and being realistic about the need to keep working hard. A year ago, they undertook a comprehensive review of all standing board committees and added working committees that complement the strategic plan of the college, the themes of which include execute the graduation contract, elevate the Spelman difference, enhance operational excellence, and promote academic innovation.[10] "Energy went sky high when we transitioned to the new committee structure," said President Campbell.

The board at Spelman has always been strong, but now they are able to begin to strategically rethink the road map for the future. There is a feeling on campus that is hard to articulate. The board and leadership recognize it and sometimes call it the "secret sauce" that gets poured into the environment in life-changing ways. Credo's vice president for student success, Michelle Samuels-Jones, captured it in the following way: "Imagine what it might feel like to live, learn, and grow in an environment that 'normalizes' expectations for women of color to achieve at the highest levels? It would feel like Spelman College: an exceptional model of a higher education institution that has hardwired its intellectual, professional, social, developmental, and spiritual culture to empower, affirm, and instill in its women, that the world is theirs to change."

---

10 "Spelman 2022: Imagine | Invent | Ascend," Spelman College, September 2018, https://www.spelman.edu/about-us/office-of-the-president/strategic-planning/strategic-plan-2022.

2. Developing Change Leaders

The new university pulls leadership up and pushes management down. The strategic vision belongs to the president, the board, and senior leaders to craft and chart. The management of the strategic plan emerging from that vision should be driven into the hands of leaders throughout the organization. Leadership has little to do with title in the new university: it has to do with initiative, ideas, action, and results. Presidents need a highly intentional set of programs to deepen the bench of leaders in every area. They must train and nurture leadership at all levels; give young or new employees opportunities for growth, development, and lateral and upward mobility; and most importantly, develop strong generalists. The new university will be a place of many multi-talented generalists and few specialists.

With this approach, traditional organizational silos and paths toward leadership in the shape of divisions, departments, and titles need to be retooled in favor of strong, ongoing, cross-functional leadership development. The new university will identify leaders at all levels—people throughout the organization who have exhibited capacity or potential to articulate and manage change. They are then mentored, empowered to lead, and supported in removing obstacles to change. Thus, leadership and the rewards that go with it are infused throughout the organization, nurtured such that the newest, along with the most seasoned, work together to implement the vision in key strategic and tactical ways.

How do you build a team of change leaders that drive an ethos of innovation throughout the university? You treat every open position as an opportunity for change leadership that pushes a university to thrive. Strategic hiring at every level can bring creative freedom and new competencies, infusing energy into teams throughout the organization. Maryville University adopted new recruitment guidelines that promote university-wide openness to change. Vice President for Student Success, Dr. Jennifer McCluskey says, "We are seeking 'drivers' who will hold people accountable, and we are consistently looking for pockets of the university where drivers are needed. We all understand that it is better to leave a position open than to settle for a candidate who is not the perfect fit." Fit for Maryville centers on two key dimensions: capacity to innovate and to build a diverse workforce. Over time, well-trained search committees have become more adept at discerning and recognizing the right-fit candidates for Maryville's culture and pace.

Presidential Hiring and Board Composition

We cannot overstate the critical importance of presidential fit in building institutional culture and developing trust with the board that facilitates action around the vision. When the opportunity for a presidential search presents itself, there are several points we recommend boards of trustees consider:

- Current search methods frequently bring two or three candidates into a final pool that becomes public and accessible to the campus for interviews. It is our contention that open searches inhibit the quality of the pools. Many effective presidents or vice presidents who are succeeding in other institutions will be hesitant to enter this type of public contest. For that reason, the pools can be shallow and prolong the process, so that both the board and the campus feel compelled to "pick one" at the end of the interviews. And yet, the right candidate might not be present. There will have to be a shift in preparation for search, contingencies for delay, and the ability to include appropriate, confidential representation from across the campus without inhibiting the best applicants.

- The board of trustees must be willing to invest the right resources in the right leader (and this applies for leaders at all levels throughout the organization). Boards need to be explicit about their desire for a leader capable of facilitating change who exhibits an intrinsic connection to and passion for the heart of the institution. These innovative candidates will require appropriately comprehensive contracts that remove distractions and allow them to focus on their critical institutional role. Clearly supporting the innovative vision of new leadership is critical to attract the kind of change leader required to guide an institution through a pivot.

- The board must be appropriately educated and prepared to own presidential hiring as the most important work they will do. With this comes the responsibility to the right candidate to cultivate readiness for transparency about the current reality of the institution, backed by data rather than intuition or anecdote. Does the board actually know what it needs to know about the health and challenges of the institution, and do they share them transparently with the top candidates in order to assess whether that leader has the fortitude, passion, and willingness to dive in? Has the board done everything in its power to unearth land mines that could inhibit a new president's success?

As important as the right-fit president is the composition of the board. When vision is clear and focused on change and risk at this level, the ability to bring it to life is dependent upon a board of trustees composed of a carefully balanced mix of individuals with aspirational networks, strategic skills, and available resources. The skills then must be actively utilized in committees focused on strategic direction. Careful board assessment and development is a necessity to ensure high levels of performance, engagement, and support for the president.

As the need for significant change made itself apparent in Marian University's darkest hours, the board faced and embraced risk, understanding that without it the university would not survive, much less thrive. Several board members knew that those risks would require a different type of leader than it had ever had. In President Elsener, they found a leader who had the courage to think innovatively and the insight to leverage the needs and energy of the city of Indianapolis. Marian's board chair emeritus, Jack Snyder, said, "There were good people on the board, and now we had a president who put us to good use. Dan brought us together around a vision for the future, and we became engaged in that vision and deployed around it effectively." As the institution reinvented itself around its Franciscan values and momentum built as each success was achieved, a unified trust in the university administration emerged from the board, and that trust has been at the crux of Marian's ability to pivot. Eighteen years later, the board harbors a deep sense of pride in what they do and the difference they can make at the university. The ability of presidents to develop their board into the institution's most passionate cheerleaders can be a game changer.

Succession Planning and Leadership Development

We have observed two trends in virtually every institution from a leadership perspective. First, most divisions within a college or university do not have leaders prepared to assume effective authority; and second, most universities do not have a prescribed set of workshops, training, and coaching designed to build such a bench. We strongly advocate for both. Succession plans that ensure the continuity of visionary and innovative leadership are essential. Every institutional vice president will need to be seriously training leadership backup. There will not be time for gaps in personnel to slow down progress. The courageous president takes time with senior staff to identify young emerging leaders, elevate them, and mentor them individually and in small groups so that the bench depth in each area drives continuous momentum even with the departure of individuals along the way. Cross-training and team-project management will need to ensure that initiatives do not fall behind. A deep, well-trained bench in every area will ensure that strategic action will go on as scheduled.

In addition, spending the time, energy, and resources to build this bench means that dozens more people become directly invested in the strategic direction of the university and in the culture of change and innovation. These mid-level leaders become drum majors and catalysts for change and innovation at all levels. And perhaps just as importantly, they see opportunities for upward and cross-area mobility that only strengthen the university.

3. Breaking Down Faculty Barriers to Innovation and Risk-Taking

We believe firmly that everyone, no matter their age or longevity in the academy, can be on the cutting edge of change. In fact, a recent meta-analysis of nearly a hundred empirical studies determined that there is no correlation between age, length of organizational employment, and the creation and implementation of innovative ideas and behavior.[11] The vast majority of university faculty do amazing work, and it is evident in the performance of our students while enrolled and particularly after they graduate. But there is a deep cultural dynamic that often undermines the ability of forward-thinking faculty to innovate and take risks: a culture of seniority, wrapped around the system of tenure. The 2016 book *Locus of Authority: The Evolution of Faculty Roles in the Governance of Higher Education* argues that "every issue facing today's colleges and universities, from stagnant degree-completion rates to worrisome cost increases, is exacerbated by a century-old system of governance that desperately requires change."[12] The new university must retool the system of tenure and challenge the culture of seniority in order to align closely with the values of student-centeredness; responsiveness to the changing needs of learners; innovation; and experimentation not only within a particular discipline, but in service to institutional vision and strategic goals. The culture of seniority can so frequently limit the expression of the innovative, entrepreneurial ideas that would allow us to meet the needs of the marketplace before us, stifle the enormous creativity of the academy, and hamper the achievement of our educational mission. The truth is that new members of our faculty will only place emphasis on cutting-edge teaching and learning if senior faculty do. If senior faculty do not, then the status quo often remains.

The senior faculty standing in judgment of their newer colleagues looking for tenure are doing so in an era of dynamic

---

11   Thomas W.H. Ng and Daniel C.Feldman, "A meta-analysis of the relationships of age and tenure with innovation related-behaviour," August 5, 2013, https://onlinelibrary.wiley.com/doi/abs/10.1111/joop.12031.

12   William G. Bowen and Eugene M.Tobin, *Locus of Authority: The Evolution of Faculty Roles in the Governance of Higher Education*, (Princeton: Princeton University Press, 2015).

change in many disciplines and in the very way teaching itself is designed. The differences in approach between new and established faculty, while not insurmountable, often can breed disconnection and miscommunication across the tenure process. Tenure decisions are made over decades—eras, really—during which the standards shift and change within the academy and among faculty. Certainly teaching, learning, and research have evolved since the implied rituals and standards that underpin tenure were developed. The requirements for and process of getting tenure creates reticence among young faculty, who become necessarily more concerned with how their senior colleagues will view their approach than whether it is truly the right strategy for student learning. As a result, those with innovative approaches to learning theory or technology feel they must water down their approaches lest they offend or irritate those who ultimately will sit on their review committees, review their tenure portfolios, and thus decide their fate. A new faculty member who brings radically different ideas into his or her teaching and learning environment is too often viewed with skepticism and resistance, or worse, as a threat to more senior members of the faculty. A recent *Chronicle of Higher Education* article focused on tenure shared the following: "Citing the ideas of George J. Stigler, the Nobel-winning economist, Ronald G. Ehrenberg, [a professor of industrial and labor relations and economics at Cornell University] says that, without tenure, senior faculty members would be in potential competition with younger colleagues and Ph.D. students for recognition and advancement, and thus might be less inclined to share what they know. With tenure, he says, 'we don't have to worry that they're going to rise up and strike us down.'"[13] This mind-set

---

13   Lee Gardner, "Want to Kill Tenure? Be Careful What You Wish For," Chronicle of Higher Education, June 18, 2018, https://www.chronicle.com/article/Want-to-Kill-Tenure-Be/243674.

lives at the heart of the problems inherent with seniority as it is—in any environment, corporate or educational, shouldn't the greatest merit be placed on the best, most impactful ideas, regardless of from whom they come?

Universities must, of course, reward achievement. But the key is, achievement for what? The answer to that question must and can only be found in our students. The new university must assign value to faculty performance insofar as it relates directly to student achievement and outcomes, specifically, how well faculty prepare students to attain their individual goals and succeed in their life's work. Particularly in our liberal arts colleges and universities, the measure of the worth of one's contributions should be centered around the ability to ideate and innovate in the service of student learning. Reorienting the reward system of an institution predominantly toward service to students would allow new student-centric ideas to rise from all areas of the institution.

The reality is that we live in an environment of rapid technological change and significant demographic shifts that require individuals and organizations to develop and adapt to new intersections between and hierarchies around knowledge and learning. The academic disciplines that make up the landscape of higher education are constantly evolving and developing. Enhanced technologies, new research discoveries, and new avenues of thought are prevalent in disciplines from biology and chemistry to business, economics, health sciences, education, history, and a host of others. For example, medical technology and learning research has pushed Marian's college of osteopathic medicine to teach differently. Lecture, data-heavy coursework, and much of the didactic learning occurs in the morning, and transitions to an afternoon of real-patient diagnosis and problem-solving connected to the morning's study topics. The technology needed to evaluate future doctors on how they treat and assess patients is integral to the training students undergo, as is the ability to interview and embrace the story of each patient. This comprehensive way to look at all angles of patient health and the distinct pedagogy needed to meet national standards has been inspirational to other departments and faculty members on campus.[14]

One of the most fundamental virtues of being an academic is committing oneself to the forward march of knowledge and understanding. Colleges and universities are marketed to prospective students and their families as places where young people can come and explore, stretch themselves, learn from and experiment with faculty who are on the cutting edge of their field. We historically have lauded universities as bastions of open expression, thought, and innovation. In fact, universities are valued precisely because of the growth that can happen for students in an environment where learning and expression is the central goal.

Given this commitment to understanding and knowledge, it makes sense that those that we charge with educating our students in higher education should be on the cutting edge, challenged in every way to keep fresh approaches to learning, teaching, and thinking front and center. More importantly, those whom we hire to design and deliver that education should be free to bring new ideas and approaches into the academy and to experiment without fear of failure. In the spirit of continual improvement, they should be free to challenge established practices, norms, ideas, or pedagogy. In order to model such values for our students, the faculty and staff of

---

14 We examine how the school of osteopathic medicine's ethos and approach has infused academic practice across the campus in the "Student at the Center" chapter.

universities should operate within an environment of exploration and change. We demand that students grow and mature throughout their intellectual journey; why not ask and demand that of ourselves? The openness to exploration and an acceptance of failure as a learning opportunity requires a vulnerability that will necessitate a strong partnership between the faculty and the administration, with a shared focus on meeting the demands of the future.

In working to create such a partnership, DWU's leadership knew that before they could introduce significant change across the institution, they needed to thoroughly and deliberately create awareness around the urgency of the institution's circumstances. They held a series of town hall meetings and shared the stark reality of the demographic numbers impacting South Dakota:

- The decline of high school graduates in the state was estimated at 15 to 20 percent.

- There were eight thousand high school graduates each year and only 60 percent of those would attend two- or four-year colleges.

- There were sixteen such institutions across the state.

- From that pool of high school graduates, after removing the subset of the 60 percent that would go out of state for their postsecondary education, each of those institutions could expect, if all enrollments were equal, approximately two hundred incoming freshmen.

The demographics alone painted a bleak picture of unsustainability for any institution not willing to invest in the quality, relevance, and visibility of its educational experience. To make such an investment, DWU's leadership needed the full support and participation of the faculty. In public addresses, President Novak drew on stories from the earliest history of the institution in the late 1800s and into the early 1900s to share the university's long-standing connection to rural innovation, including early commitments to satellite campuses near Native American reservations and across South Dakota, Nebraska, and Montana. She posed the question: given our mission and our history, what are our core competencies, and where can we both bring the most value to our students and truly excel in our work? Collectively, the campus community determined that agility and innovation were two of the institution's greatest strengths. With a commitment to those two values, they began to explicitly recognize them both in general review and reward processes, and in the tenure process in a variety of ways, including:

- **Adoption of new pedagogies:** DWU consistently recognizes faculty members that contribute to innovative pedagogy and has also recognized the valuable learning created by failure when taking this type of risk. There is a place for reflection in the tenure evaluation on what failures that faculty has experienced in their teaching, and what learning and change those challenging experiences yielded.

- **Professional development:** Furthering one's own learning and development through training aligned specifically with strategic initiatives is considered during the tenure process, and the institution invests in that development accordingly. For example, faculty who participated in training at Apple's Cupertino headquarters or in digital workshops held by Apple leaders on campus related to Digital DWU's Initiative can feature that in their tenure applications.

We have witnessed President Novak's continuous efforts to praise the campus community and remind them what they have done and are doing to rise above the competition, contributing to high levels of motivation and commitment on behalf of the faculty across the institution.

4. Abandoning Consensus and Reimagining Committees

In the new university, consensus across stakeholder groups does not precede action, but follows it. Actions and initiatives in the form of pilot programs are essential to try new approaches, to question long-held assumptions, and to demonstrate to the community what is truly possible. Abandoning the elusive goal of consensus allows for the creation of ongoing inclusive opportunities for engagement and the acceleration of new ideas that, through trial and error, can propel the mission and vision of the institution forward. Future-oriented leadership charts a course and engages key visionaries to help shape the institution's path in alignment with their goals. Once that course is initiated and progress is achieved, then consensus will build around the success.

> In the new university, consensus across stakeholder groups does not precede action, but follows it.

If leaders clearly present a strong vision that is relevant at a macro-organizational level, they can continue to build momentum despite any tactical setbacks, and consensus will evolve. In any organization, there will always be those who disagree with an approach. Effective initiatives are often critiqued solely because either consensus was not reached, or consultation was not requested. Debate is a healthy intellectual exercise to be valued but is not an end in and of itself. Disagreement is never—ever—a reason to not act. There can be no vetoes over courageous innovation. For presidents in particular, an overreliance on consensus-building, often in fear of the dreaded vote of no-confidence, has a chilling effect on bold, courageous decision-making, frequently miring the university in endless stakeholder input but little measurable action via committees.

Committees, staples of the traditional university, can devolve into groups of well-meaning faculty and staff who begin to water down initiatives, critique change, and ultimately avoid significant decisions in favor of incrementalism. Often it is the very nature of these committee meetings that sets them up for failure: how can anything but incrementalism emerge from one-hour blocks of time each month or quarter? In our respective careers, we have seen dozens of committees devolve into unending processing. We see precious energy and valuable time wasted, transformed into weariness and disengagement. Frequently, the faculty or staff most engaged in and enthusiastic about change and experimentation who serve on such committees quit them out of frustration. Committees at their worst ensure that any decision is slowed in such a way that it can never significantly alter the culture. The simple truth is that in the heterogeneous culture of the university, the myriad student, faculty, and staff perspectives means that there is no consensus on any significant issue. Therefore, we must rethink the way we gather stakeholder input and how and in what ways we incorporate it. Many colleges and universities are now doing their best planning work in summit format, allotting a full day to encourage creative strategies to become fully formed, decisions to be made, and clear action assigned. Committees work best when membership is fluid and rotating, and when the chairperson is organized, action-oriented, and committed to results.

In the most innovative universities, the very best strategic work done by committees is accomplished when their mission is clear and directly related to the priorities of the institution, and when the value of speed is embedded and non-negotiable. Committees need enforceable deadlines for results and clear goals and objectives. Maryville University chairman of the board, Thomas Boudreau, said, "Everyone else has access to all of the other things we do, and none if it is proprietary. We have two strategic advantages, speed and agility." Although speed and agility may be intimidating to many of us in academia, our ability to anticipate and react to change in higher education will define how we succeed in the future. Maryville has embraced a deadline-oriented culture—consensus among leaders from across campus that stalls a deadline is simply not an option. Whether it is a new program, a policy decision, or a new residence-life initiative, a deadline for implementation is set and adhered to. The results are the reward. Often those results come in job satisfaction, growth, and revenue. Everyone likes to support a winning initiative. Regardless, results provide fuel for the next strategic move. With focus and anticipation, deliberating an idea or program need not be a long march to inaction but rather, a decisive seizure of opportunity.

Perhaps most importantly, courageous leadership begins with the president. Presidents must lead with courage and embrace the fundamental truth that they are chosen by the board to take risks, innovate, and challenge the status quo. The average university of today *must* change, and as such, the president should proudly play the role of Disrupter-in-Chief. The president is, and should intentionally be, chosen and positioned to lead, craft, and manage that change, with a committed group of professionals and advisors from all areas of the academy. A culture of risk-taking and innovation embraces the realities of today's higher-education environment and connects the entire institutional community in the march to one overarching vision: a relevant, sustainable, student-centered university. Presidents and the leaders they empower throughout the institution must embody courage each and every day, and they must not fear disagreement, rejection, or failure. Isn't this courage what we wish for our students to embrace and apply in the world once they leave us? It is a gift to them to model the change we seek.

Courageous Leadership: Championing Disruption, Risk, and Innovation Challenge Questions

- Is at least one critical constituency at your institution (board, leadership team, faculty, staff) consistently focused on and pushing for change and new ways of thinking?

- Are your institution's committees streamlined, functional, and effective at the tasks to which they are dedicated?

- Does your institution celebrate and reward risk-taking?

- Does your culture reward continuous internal learning and experimentation for faculty and staff?

- Is the search for consensus an obstacle to agility and innovation at your institution?

- Are your board members chosen strategically for skill in areas needed for institutional health?

- Does your board own and share the vision of the institution?

- Are your board members being educated about the future of learning through regular board development?

- Has your board of trustees assessed itself for readiness to address the trends exerting pressure on higher education over the next ten years?

- Is your president sufficiently protected through the support of the board of trustees to be an agent of change?

- Does your leadership team focus on strategic issues at least 50 percent of the time?

- Do the members of your institution's leadership team all understand the pivotal issues in the future of higher education?

- Are you developing leaders for innovation, risk-taking, and experimentation at all levels, including among associate vice presidents, deans, and directors?

- Does your faculty leadership understand the relevance of new learning paradigms?

- Are faculty and staff being prepared for the future of learning?

- Does tenure at your institution inhibit innovation and experimentation?

- Does the faculty-evaluation process reflect a focus on student outcomes, innovative pedagogy, and contribution to institutional mission?

The Student at the Center: Transforming Learning for the Future

Think of family members, friends, and coworkers who have demonstrated that they could attain amazing heights and unlock enormous talent but struggled to do so within the constructs of a formal education. Some of the most transformational, innovative minds of our era—Steve Jobs, Bill Gates, and Mark Zuckerberg, to name but three—dropped out of college and built new worlds in their garages and living rooms that have created, in large part, the world of technology in which we now live, and to which we as educators must now respond.[15] The irony is not lost on us. These individuals, like so many of our students, have innate potential that often cannot be unleashed in a traditional classroom setting.

---

15   Abigail Hess,"10 Ultra-Successful Millionaire and Billionaire College Dropouts," CNBC Make It, May 10, 2017, https://www.cnbc.com/2017/05/10/10-ultra-successful-millionaire-and-billionaire-college-dropouts.html.

The hundreds or thousands of students we welcome to our campuses each year are each unique, with different ways of interacting, communicating, and thinking. Through exhaustive ongoing research into human genetics and brain development, we know that they, like all people, process information, absorb concepts, and commit knowledge to memory differently. Despite all their rich and valuable differences, we bring these students together into classes most often oriented around one way of digesting information, with a professor in front of the classroom imparting his or her knowledge. We then measure the students' success based largely on whether they can adapt to that singular mode of learning.

The challenge before us as educators committed to the success of our students is to rebuild our instructional models and learning spaces around the learner's vantage point rather than our own. To do this, we must draw on what we can explore

The students of the future will rely on us to meet them as they are, not as we are.

about the way different individuals approach learning, utilizing a foundation of integrated, accessible data that allows for rich and timely student support. The information and tools to undertake this rebuilding are readily available. While the work is complex and requires culture change, this transformation is urgently needed: the students of the future will rely on us to meet them as they are, not as we are.

Since antiquity, education has been organized around the lecture. The central assumption in this mode of delivery was that learned individuals possessed the content in their heads through years of study, analysis, and commitment to their disciplines. If you wanted to access that content, you had to become a student and sit at their feet, listen, and transcribe. This dissemination of content was based on two principles: ownership of knowledge and a particular way of learning. Listen, write everything down, memorize it, recite it back, and if you were committed and perceptive enough, you too could be a scholar charged with lecturing to the next generation of emerging students. As other forms of knowledge began to develop, the lecture made its way into math, science, and other evolving disciplines. This method has not fundamentally changed for over twenty-five hundred years. Even the advent and implementation of some forms of technology have not shaken the lecture's iron grip on teaching. Universities place students in classes with content experts and expect them to learn based solely through the way we teach. If the way those students learn happens to be different from how we teach, he or she must seek help, hire tutors, or undertake remedial work.

Even at institutions with small faculty-to-student ratios, the geography of classrooms is largely still designed with a "front" of the room, where the teacher is stationed. Rows of seats and desks are arranged so that students can focus on the instructor. Technology is still largely utilized to continue a one-way dissemination of content and not used to actively engage the learner. This approach will not achieve the goal of making learning more accessible to more types of students. In fact, it does the opposite. It isolates students, rather than linking them to others in ways that allow for the kind of problem-solving activities that reflect the reality of the professional world.

However, we now have decades of research at our disposal to change traditional learning constructs and move toward a deeply personalized model. We have access to rich, endless content at all times through technology that is always with us, as well as volumes of research that direct us to a more complex and nuanced understanding of the human brain and how it works. We now also possess an opportunity to collect and strategically use extensive data to shape individual learning journeys in partnership with our students. The new university's responsibility is twofold: first, it must adapt the role of faculty and the learning spaces in which they teach to a new reality of how information and knowledge flow through the world; and second, it must include the student as not only an active participant, but also a co-creator of their own learning experience. We will examine two critical needs in reshaping learning at our institutions:

1. **Navigating the changing role of faculty and learners**: The democratization of knowledge, i.e., the broad, fingertip availability of vast amounts of content previously held by scholars and imparted to students, has an extraordinary impact on the context within which learners enter the collegiate environment and influences how teachers must shift from owners of knowledge to facilitators of discernment. Additionally, scientific research about brain development and ways of effectively connecting information to different types of learners offer rich opportunities to reimagine how we physically and instructionally craft learning experiences to accommodate and celebrate a variety of approaches.

2. **Using data to create personalized learning journeys:** The ability to collect a broad variety of data in real time about our students from the minute they join our institution (or even from the moment we become aware of them as prospects) offers us the opportunity both to identify how our students learn most effectively and track the progress of their learning. Moreover, mapping their

progress can directly impact their success, streamlining systems in tandem to centralize information and appropriately distribute student support.

1. Navigating the Changing Role of Faculty and Learners

Consider the incredible explosion of information that the internet and digital technology has wrought. Everyone with a smartphone now carries a library in his or her pocket. We collectively perform 1.2 trillion searches a year on Google alone—that's forty thousand per second. More data has been created in the past two years than in the entire previous history of the human race.[16] The democratization of knowledge across our society has vast implications for the role of faculty, for the definition of teaching, and for the way we measure and assess student achievement. Make no mistake, trained professors are vital to the learning process in higher education, as they can guide a student's journey from limited knowledge and awareness to understanding, application, discernment, and critical problem-solving; but the learner, not the teacher, exists at the center of the personalized-learning model. Universities were the keepers of knowledge for a long time, but we must now act as agile facilitators of that knowledge. Our ability to serve students in this capacity is completely dependent upon our ability to change how learning happens at our institutions.

Additionally, when we consider the individual student, thanks to brain and learning research and the application of science and technology, we know a great deal more about how his or her brain develops. Gender, body chemistry, pace of growth, and genetics

---

16   Bernard Marr, "Big Data: 20 Mind-Boggling Facts Everyone Must Read," Forbes, September 30, 2015,https://www.forbes.com/sites/bernardmarr/2015/09/30/big-data-20-mind-boggling-facts-everyone-must-read/#b8339d917b1e.

all impact brain development as children. We also know that external factors such as parenting, environment, diet, exercise— even trauma—influence this development. In fact, we now know that brain development changes over time based on a variety of external stimuli, including exposure to and use of technology such as television, cell phones, computers, and the like. In other words, how information is presented and how people's brains process that information will determine if they effectively understand and retain it.

Working together, life coaches, learning designers, and faculty in the new university will craft experiences within courses that allow for personalized instruction. A personalized approach is one where all students are moving through their own journeys of discovery, taking in and absorbing information and ideas based on their own learning strengths, with faculty as periodic caretakers and facilitators along that journey. This approach will not guarantee students' success, but it will give them the best opportunity to present what they do know and understand. Each student experiments, innovates, tries, fails, learns, adapts, and ultimately masters areas of study, and then moves on. In this model, learning is an integrated, interconnected ecosystem where everything impacts everything else.

In support of the new roles of faculty and students alike in a personalized-learning model, learning spaces will change to be flexible, mobile, and integrated. Learning in the new university happens everywhere, because mobile technology (smart-phones, tablets, and other tools) allows students to engage more thoroughly in the learning process and move beyond the artificial constraints of a classroom. Learning spaces and places must break down a student's isolation and connect him or her with his or her fellow students and the broad world of experience and knowledge through group orientation and collaborative problem-solving. These types of learning spaces necessitate a high level of connectivity across campus. Learning happens everywhere, therefore access to learning must be ubiquitous. Classrooms, libraries, study areas, and the like become fused into one great learning space where students engage in the learning journey. In the new university, the most acclaimed approaches see the entire campus as one free-flowing learning space.[17] Our pivoting institutions have approached personalized learning in a variety of ways.

Maryville's Active-Learning Ecosystem

Maryville's Vice President for Integrated Marketing and Communications Marcia Sullivan characterizes their approach to students in the following way: "We are loyal to our students above all history, tradition, pedagogy, and comfort." At the most strategic levels, the entire institution is geared toward improving student outcomes inside and outside the classroom. In order to accomplish the strategic plan and to create a culture of continuous innovation in and outside of the classroom, Maryville looked carefully at teaching and learning, and in partnership with Apple, built an Active Learning Ecosystem (A.L.E.) around three interlocking components: life coaching, learning design, and the digital world.[18]

The A.L.E., developed initially in 2014 and continually evolving and growing, is predicated on the fundamental assumption, which we've discussed here, that all students learn and process information differently and thus require personalized learning facilitated by the

---

17   Diana G. Oblinger, (Editor), *Learning Spaces* (Louisville: EDUCAUSE, 2006).

18   The life-coaching and learning-design components of the A.L.E. are explored later in this chapter and in the "Explosion of Adult Education" chapter, respectively.

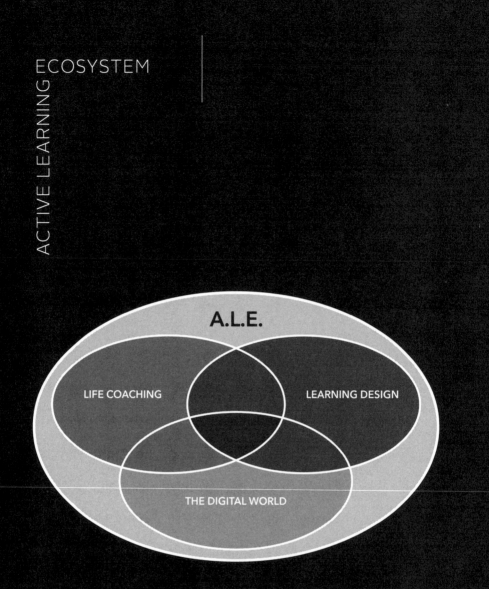

A.L.E.

LIFE COACHING

LEARNING DESIGN

THE DIGITAL WORLD

In partnership with Apple, Maryville built an Active Learning Ecosystem in which faculty members partner with learning designers and life coaches to create robust learning content and connections across the student experience facilitated by technology.

most relevant technology. Applied learning embedded in the A.L.E. means a student's knowledge of a subject is based on their ability to apply what they know and understand in order to address real problems in that field. If students can grasp and apply the elements of basic psychology, why should they spend a year taking the two-course sequence of Psych 101 and 102?

The central key to the A.L.E. is that the pace of learning must be self-determined, not artificially divided into eight semesters over four years. It is a model that takes the core principles of the Montessori experience[19] and merges them with the latest in learning diagnostics and technology to free students and their faculty facilitators in ways the old format has not done and could not do.

Maryville's A.L.E. uses learning diagnostics and learning theory to build intricate profiles on all traditional undergraduate students, showing how and why they learn the way they do. Utilizing those profiles, faculty members partner with learning designers to create curriculum and robust learning content that connects with students on a one-to-one level. The facilitative tool or delivery system for this instruction is the iPad, which opens up multiple resources and learning approaches in the same space and time.

Maryville launched its Digital World initiative in partnership with Apple in 2015, when over six hundred iPads were deployed to incoming freshman and faculty. The iPad, however, was simply a tool to facilitate a redesign and reimagining of pedagogy across the institution. The paradigm shift around digital learning was adopted initially by what Maryville calls their pied pipers: a small group of visionary faculty and learning designers who developed an approach

---

19 Austin Matte, "Montessori: The New Science Behind a Century-Old Methodology (Part 1)," Learning and the Brain, June 11, 2017, https://www.learningandthebrain. com/blog/montessori-the-new-science-behind-a-century-old-methodology/.

rooted in learning theory, based on personalized instruction, and focused on problem-solving, which they then took campus-wide through training and facilitation. Students are told that Digital World classes represent "a collaboration between learner and professor. All of the world's information is just one online search away, so our professors are adapting the way they teach. Digital World classes will have you working together with professors and your fellow students to tackle real-world challenges ... which is ideal preparation for the job that awaits you after graduation."

Faculty at Maryville have embraced the Digital World initiative and say that it has been a game-changer for how they teach. For example:

- Professors for introductory science courses—content-heavy, challenging classes—rely on feedback from adaptive-learning software to tailor course content to help more students effectively master the topics at hand.

- In a literature class, students use their iPads to create their own children's literature to take into their practicum classrooms and read to their own students, in turn teaching young learners how to create and publish e-books.

- The high levels of engagement around the Digital World initiative led to the development of an application-development minor, which is open to students in any major, in order to allow them to build coding and development skills.

Today, more than four thousand iPads are deployed to all undergraduate students, faculty, and a cadre of adjuncts, and the new pedagogy has taken hold. One faculty member says, "The future of iPads in the classroom at Maryville is tremendous. We are putting students in a place where they can be the creative innovators for tomorrow."[20]

DWU'S Learn Strong Program and High-Relevance Core

DWU took a different approach to shaping the learning journey of its students, developing a general-education curriculum focused on preparing students for twenty-first century leadership and digital competency and aligning it with relevance for DWU's geographic area and South Dakota's economic drivers. At the heart of the new core lived the Learn Strong program, a series of courses focused on helping students discern their strengths and equip them with the necessary skills to become successful employees. Outcomes of participation in the Learn Strong program include the student:

- developing an understanding of his or herself and others using the language of Clifton StrengthsFinder,

- understanding and committing to personal behaviors that promote wellbeing in his or herself and others,

- communicating effectively in personal and professional settings,

- creating and making effective presentations in formal settings,

- discerning and articulating his or her vocation, and

- understanding and managing budgets.[21]

20 "Digital World Maryville," Maryville University, August 2018, https://www.maryville.edu/digitalworld/.

21 "The Learn Strong program is your basis for success," Dakota Wesleyan University, August 2018, https://www.dwu.edu/academics/learn-strong.

The Learn Strong program embraced a holistic approach to education by developing professional communication and numeracy skills, honing leadership dispositions such as teamwork, ethical decision-making, resiliency, conflict resolution, and learning from failure through applied activities, role playing and simulations; as well as a series of breadth-of-knowledge courses designed to allow students to practically apply current issues to an understanding of scientific literacy, personal and professional financial literacy, civic engagement, and humanics. The four-year Learn Strong program complemented the academic-skill development acquired through the general-education program, the co-curricular experiences of the students, and the student's major program of study. Specific focus on resume writing and graduate-school preparation was complemented by mock interviews for each student with President Novak and community members. Sessions on professional networking, apartment leasing, health insurance considerations, paying student loan debt, and general post-college survivor skills were all embedded into the required program.

Six years after the initial launch of the Learn Strong program, the university faculty acted with responsiveness to the needs of the region by redesigning the core curriculum once again. Faculty from across the institution's academic programs have collaborated on this interdisciplinary approach to develop leaders equipped with the problem-solving and project-management skills vital to success. Beginning in the fall of 2016, all students were enrolled in a core freshman course called "Interdisciplinary Investigations: Creativity and Innovation." In this first course, students receive an introduction to the basic principles of innovation and project management as they identify and engage with a real community problem, develop and design possible solutions, then test, plan, and implement a strategy.

One particularly unique component of this course is the tolerance for failure. South Dakota, like the larger Great Plains regional economy, is largely comprised of small and medium enterprises developed by local entrepreneurs. This spirit tolerates, and even encourages, failure as a mechanism for learning and improving. Within this freshman course, students are encouraged to see failure as a growth opportunity, and explore questions such as:

- What is conceptual creativity and how can we apply it now?

- How do we discern and apply patterns and connections between seemingly disconnected subjects?

- How do we apply the three-step innovation process of ideation, identification, and implementation?

- How do we influence others to take interest in our ideas and to apply them?

- How do teams negotiate and compromise between several potentially good ideas?

- How and why do we pursue multiple solutions to a problem?

- When is it best to work in groups? When is it best to work alone?

- What makes an effective team, especially when there is no appointed leader?[22]

The second core course during the sophomore or junior year encourages the students to build upon these competencies by

---

22 "Interdisciplinary Investigations: Creativity and Innovation," (course syllabus), Dakota Wesleyan University, 2018.

engaging in specific leadership development alongside a community-based service-learning project. Working in teams, students can employ their leadership strengths and reflect on team dynamics, leveraging their knowledge and assets and those of the community partner to engage in an improvement project.

Spelman's Metacognitive Study

With research and data-informed strategies, Spelman looks deeply at the identity, cultural background, and learning strengths of its students. They deliberately dig into the issues of readiness and assessment in order to prescribe the learning journey for each of their students. Their intense focus on this area is such that they have received federal grant funding to study metacognitive learning and how it affects Black women. Metacognition refers to the "processes used to plan, monitor, and assess one's understanding and performance," and includes "a critical awareness of a) one's thinking and learning and b) oneself as a thinker and learner."[23] Spelman Provost and Vice President for Academic Affairs, Sharon L. Davies, said, "We are aware that this is a new generation of learners who will have lived their lives without ever having to consult a library and want to make sure that this does not give them a false sense of depth and expertise."

All entering first-year and most transfer students enroll in Spelman's signature African Diaspora and the World (ADW) course, which is designed for students to examine the major themes associated with the African Diaspora within a global context and from perspectives that are both interdisciplinary and gender-informed. The ADW course operates on the belief that it is important

---

23 Nancy Chick, "Metacognition," Vanderbilt University Center for Teaching, accessed October 15, 2018, https://cft.vanderbilt.edu/guides-sub-pages/metacognition/.

to understand the relations between thinking, reading, and writing. To that end, learning experiences and activities in ADW require close reading, critical thinking, and communication of comprehension through oral and written work. Spelman is using a randomized controlled trial led by an interdisciplinary team of cognitive and social scientists to assess the impact of metacognitive teaching methods on ADW course participants and will conduct a parallel second study of peer-tutors and their clients. Study results could transform pedagogical practices for faculty, peer-tutors, and students in all discipline areas.

Beyond such course development and pedagogical research, three additional critical initiatives are underway at Spelman to deepen the personalization of each student's learning:

- They have gathered a team to talk seriously about summer readiness programs. Aimed at increasing the success of Spelman students by filling preparation gaps, pre-matriculation readiness programs engage the faculty around developing a deeper understanding of how to meet new students where they are and take them to higher levels of learning.

- They are reviewing advising and mentoring procedures and applicable tools to increase effectiveness in these areas. Looking carefully at predictive analytics, they are making investments to increase the availability of integrated, real-time data.

- They are also assuming greater responsibility for collecting longitudinal information about students after they graduate. That information will correspond to metrics on each major area of study. Changes to programs and curriculum will occur accordingly.

Marian's Medical College Transformation

Marian defines a great Catholic university as one that educates transformational leaders for service to the world. The power of mission, faith, and sense of service to humanity is felt on campus. The campus community uses what they call the "holy trinity" template to guide the creation, funding, and implementation of new programs and strategic initiatives. The three interlocking circles call them to focus on the needs in the community and the world; the vision, mission, passion, and historical competence of Marian; and the economic engine that will fuel and sustain the initiatives.

By using their holy trinity template, they saw the great need for more physicians in Indiana. Despite a robust higher educational landscape in the state, Indiana had only one medical school at a large public institution and ranked thirty-eighth in the country for physician density. Marian put out a bold vision to start a medical school in Indiana and began to raise the necessary funds and build partnerships with area hospital systems. With the launch of its college of osteopathic medicine in 2013, fueled by more than 60 million dollars in donations from private individuals and health care systems, Marian became the first Roman Catholic institution in the country to open a medical school and significantly expanded learning opportunities for medical students in Indiana.[24] In 2017, they graduated the first class of physicians, and in doing so have made the institution an invaluable economic resource in the state.

---

24 Carolyn Schierhorn, "Indiana Takes Aim at Physician Shortfall with New Osteopathic Medical School," The DO, March 2012, https://thedo.osteopathic. org/2012/03/indiana-takes-aim-at-physician-shortfall-with-new-osteopathic-medical-school/.

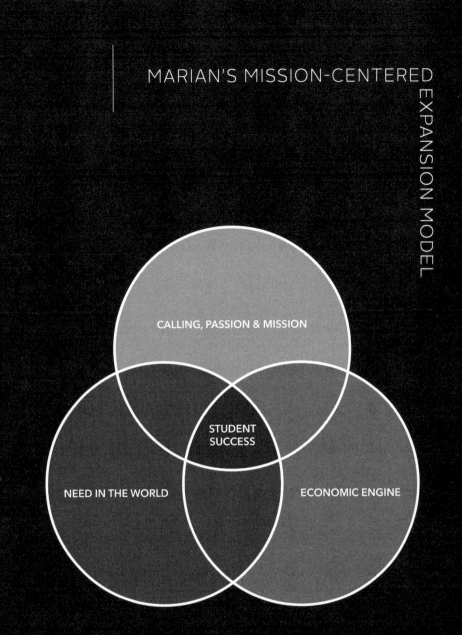

The three interlocking circles call Marian University to focus on the needs of the community and the world; the vision, mission, passion, and historical competence of Marian; and the economic engine that will fuel and sustain the initiatives.

The holistic, innovative approach of the field of osteopathic medicine itself has provided unexpected and welcome challenges to reimagine teaching and learning in other areas of the institution. Osteopathy focuses around a practical, hands-on, whole-person approach to wellness, finding and addressing underlying causes of physical pain and illness. Doctors of osteopathic medicine "pride themselves on their emphasis on preventive medicine, a patient-centered, holistic approach to care, and patient empowerment to strive toward the body's natural, optimal state of structure/function, and self-healing and health. They also utilize diagnosis of and manual manipulation of the neuromusculoskeletal system and stress its interconnectedness with every other organ system in the body."[25] The translation of osteopathy's approach into other schools across the Marian campus has been remarkable, with faculty and staff recognizing and embracing the value of a student-success-centered, holistic, wellness-oriented focus. In addition to changes in the nursing, sciences, and business pedagogy to better reflect the values inherent in the osteopathic tradition, a few specific initiatives are underway to deepen the integration and adoption of more holistic education:

Leadership

Once the college of osteopathic medicine was off and running, Marian had a board retreat to discuss the next big need in the world that they could pursue. Through research and discussion with leaders in education, business, health care, not-for-profits, and other enterprises, they discovered the greatest need across industry was for

---

25 Patrick Wu and Jonathan Siu, "A Brief Guide to Osteopathic Medicine," American Association of Colleges of Osteopathic Medicine, April 2015, https://www.aacom.org/docs/default-source/cib/bgom.pdf.

exceptional leadership. Marian University committed to developing transformational leaders for service to the world. They define leaders as those who are inquisitive and knowledgeable; skilled in both professional and executive-functioning abilities (multiculturalism, communication, etc.); trustworthy; and physically, emotionally, and spiritually healthy.[26] They are building this commitment to leadership in all curricular, co-curricular, and external areas so that Marian graduates are truly distinctive in their leadership abilities.

Teacher Preparation

Marian Klipsch Educator's College started a newly designed teacher-preparation program in the 2018–2019 academic year designed to offer students a bachelor's-plus-master's degree program that can be completed in eight to ten semesters, featuring a one-year paid teaching and mentoring residency with supervised training to work with students in high-needs schools; early, frequent classroom experience; a competency-based, skills-mastery outcomes focus; and a study abroad experience in a high-performing school. The deeply experiential and supported nature of this program, along with its focus on developing competencies and skill mastery, align it well with the very best in innovation in higher education, and with the holistic values of the college of osteopathy.

Two-Year College

Significantly, in the fall of 2019, Marian will open a new and innovative two-year college. President Elsener says that this initiative "fits well the university's mission as a Catholic university

---

26 Daniel J. Elsener, "What Does it Mean to be a Transformational Leader?" The Marian University Blog, July 2017, https://www.marian.edu/blog/blog/2017/07/17/what-does-it-mean-to-be-a-transformational-leader.

and its relentless effort to bring educational options that are effective in meeting the needs of diverse student populations." The university is aligning itself with the Lumina Foundation in this project. "The Lumina Foundation's goal of increasing the proportion of Americans with high-quality degrees, certificates, and other credentials to 60 percent by 2025 will not be achieved if higher education maintains the status quo," President Elsener said:

"We require revolutionary responses that address the populations of students who aren't going to college or aren't finishing. Over the past two years, Marian University contracted an outside consultant to conduct a feasibility study around launching a two-year college, and subsequently assembled an implementation task force of faculty, staff and trustees to determine the best way to roll it out. Our innovative and mission-driven two-year college will provide the sense of community, support systems, and professional opportunities that many students need for success beyond high school.

"The college will be small, enrolling seventy-five to 125 students who will study in areas that are relevant to employers and aligned with Marian University's mission. Beginning with associate-degree programs in liberal arts, information technology, and business, Marian will continue to add programs as the economy and employers' needs shift. Personal one-to one mentoring will enrich the student experience, along with strong partnerships with central-Indiana companies to create clear pipelines for employment. The intent is for these partnerships, along with state and federal funding, to allow a student to complete the program with little to no debt."

With all these initiatives, Marian has kept their focus on what the community needs, designed programs that meet these needs and the learning needs of identified students and has done so with agility and speed.

2. Using Data to Create Personalized Learning Journeys

The role that data has come to play in the management and individualization of our daily lives and experiences is an essential consideration in any conversation about how we use data on our campuses. The emergence of Facebook, Google, and Amazon has essentially placed the collection of data on steroids, with the sum of accumulated data doubling every several months,[27] constantly generating information about ourselves and the world within which we live. In turn, the application of data analytics to this avalanche of information has, by discerning patterns of behavior across a variety of areas of human endeavor, ushered in a whole new era in work, study, and life. The evolution of big data makes it not only an important tool for higher education but also, increasingly, an important professional field of study for students.

Embracing this reality, in 2018, Dakota Wesleyan University rolled out their digital initiative, which will extend across both the curriculum and the co-curriculum. It is their hope that it will change the way every student works and learns from the classroom to the football field to project-based experiences. It is an initiative that recognizes how technology can be leveraged to develop more engaged learners, while simultaneously equipping them for the realities of their workplace. Ninety-three percent of industry leaders engaged in an innovation summit at DWU indicated that technology was radically changing the nature of their industry. This trend

---

27 "The Zettabyte Era: Trends and Analysis," Cisco Systems, June 2017, https://www.cisco.com/c/en/us/solutions/collateral/service-provider/visual-networking-index-vni/vni-hyperconnectivity-wp.html.

ignited the Digital DWU initiative designed to equip students with the literacy necessary to use technology wisely to analyze data, review analytics to inform decision-making, understand the ethically responsible use of technology, and discern relevant information for use in solving problems and identifying new opportunities. Faculty have been technologically equipped to engage in professional development around new digital pedagogies at the highest possible levels.

A widening chasm exists broadly, though, between our industry's recognition of how central data and data analytics have become to our lives and our institutional capabilities around and commitment to the truly strategic collection and use of data to improve the student experience. For decades, we have collected a wealth of information from our students and families through the admissions process, residential living, curricular and co-curricular experiences, advising, and campus engagement—yet we do not convey that data across the student's learning experience, instead leaving staff and faculty who cross that student's path in the future to discover (or not discover) his or her individual history. Connecting that data across various institutional silos such that it can be effectively aggregated and analyzed has never been systematically accomplished. This isolation of information has not been a conscious policy but rather a weakness born of institutional silos with insular loyalty, poor cross-functional lines of communication, and an inability or unwillingness to fully utilize our available technological systems. In a time when much of the attention of the academy has turned needed attention to student success and retention rates, there is a huge gap in our ability to assess students correctly, teach them effectively, and help them apply their learning in a relevant way.

Accomplishing the goal of strategically using data for student success requires addressing the issue of antiquated data-management systems that were largely created in the 1980s and 1990s and have not been adequately redesigned and redeployed on our campuses. How many times, when administrators across the academy have wanted to discuss an issue (the reasons for retention, the matriculation rates for students from various socioeconomic or ethnic/racial backgrounds, the revenue generated by academic and athletic programs, etc.), have people had to go to several areas, extract the data, and create new reports? Often this process can take days or even weeks to perform. Gathering the requested data at an institution is often more akin to an archeological dig.

In the new university, use of real-time student data supported by a comprehensive software platform unlocks the potential of each learner, allowing faculty and staff to recognize and maximize a student's individual journey of intellectual and social development. Strategic use of data becomes the connective tissue around which the entire life cycle of the student revolves. Increasingly, institutions are turning to complex and customizable tools like SalesForce to begin integrating data. The result is a single, horizontal platform where data can be shared and analyzed, and tools, resources, and experiences can be designed and brought to bear for each student. If we think of the span of engagement of any student as stretching from recruitment by admissions, through matriculation, in-class and out-of-class learning, living situation, student advising, career services, and alumni relations, there are millions of data points along

> Strategic use of data becomes the connective tissue around which the entire life cycle of the student revolves.

that journey. All of this valuable knowledge will be collected and analyzed for patterns of activity and used for real-time service response. Georgia State University's "GPS Advising" system, for example, monitors every student's academic progress in real time through complex computer algorithms, analyzing data points, notifying advisors if an individual student's performance is slipping, and triggering the expectation that the advisor will set up a meeting to examine any issues and be of help. In the 2014–2015 academic year, forty-three thousand such meetings were generated. The resulting improvements in student completion, especially among underrepresented students, is astounding: between 2003 and 2015, African-American student graduation rates rose from 29 to 57 percent; from 22 to 54 percent for Hispanic students; and Pell-eligible student completion rose to non-Pell student completion rates.[28] One student says, "The advisors here are really invested in their students. They're really into making sure you're okay. It motivates you to really try harder, because you know somebody is backing you up."

In short, data can build the DNA of student success. The structure of that DNA means that students can receive services, counseling, and assistance in anticipation of challenge or distress—not weeks or months after issues have emerged. It allows education, teaching, counseling, and other services to be tailored and personalized to the student. This will allow a student to understand his or her own patterns of behavior and learning strengths and to develop skills and abilities to mitigate their weaknesses. Students will be able to own their own progress and understand who they are and why they succeed or struggle in various contexts.

---

28 Nick Chiles, "At Georgia State, more black students graduate each year than at any U.S. college," The Hechinger Report, November 26, 2016, https://hechingerreport.org/at-georgia-state-black-students-find-comfort-and-academic-success/.

Centralized Data, Distributed Student Support

Additionally, connecting data in the right ways across silos and ensuring appropriate reporting of that data allows us to most appropriately disseminate student outreach and support to those with greatest expertise, because knowledge about each student's challenges and successes is evident and available. Faculty, financial-aid officers, residence-life staff, and other staff that interact regularly with students can see both a relevant holistic picture of a student's journey (with all appropriate privacy measures in place; the examination of the use of data and its impacts on student privacy in higher education and, more broadly, privacy law, is complex and ongoing. See the following two footnotes for an article and a report that explore two facets of that examination.[29]) and the specific pieces of information immediately relevant to that faculty or staff's role. For example, as students have come to college less prepared and in need of greater support, we all know that the traditional faculty-advising model must be reengineered.[30] In the new university, faculty will no longer be advisors across the spectrum of the collegiate experience, but rather mentors about what they know best: i.e., their field of study and a student's preparation for entry into that field. Meanwhile, with the addition of student-success or life coaches, students have dedicated resources holistically connected to their

---

29   Andrew Giambrone,"When Big Data Meets the Blackboard," *The Atlantic*, June 22, 2015, https://www.theatlantic.com/education/archive/2015/06/big-data-student-privacy/396452/; Andrew Ho, "Advancing Educational Research and Student Privacy in the 'Big Data' Era," National Academy of Education, 2017, https://naeducation.org/wp-content/uploads/2017/05/Ho-FINAL.pdf.

30   Sara Butrymowicz, "Most colleges enroll students who are not prepared for college," PBS News Hour, January 30, 2017, https://www.pbs.org/newshour/education/colleges-enroll-students-arent-prepared-higher-education; Michael Anft, "Student Needs Have Changed. Advising Must Change, Too," The Chronicle of Higher Education, July 1, 2018, https://www.chronicle.com/article/Student-Needs-Have-Changed/243797.

entire collegiate experience, ready to help them navigate challenges and opportunities around and beyond the classroom experience.

Maryville has chosen to embrace a dedication to life coaching. Life coaches are equipped with an extraordinary depth and breadth of data about the students they serve and act as a partner in each student's collegiate experience. The students are coached from the beginning of their journey until they choose an academic advisor just before their junior year. Life coaches work with their student partners ten times each semester—a far cry from the once-a-semester course-selection model of advising. Each life coach at Maryville:

- delivers personalized coaching services through innovative and proactive outreach to approximately ninety new incoming first-year students, with availability to help any student in need of assistance in order to ensure a positive student experience;

- creates a multitude of ways to provide high touch support for students in overcoming obstacles, gaining confidence, and reaching their goals (e.g., weekly meetings, texts, blogs, push notifications);

- serves as a key player in the social and academic integration for first-year students by developing a positive rapport with students, parents, faculty, and staff;

- maintains thorough and accurate student information on attendance, participation, progress, retention, graduation, and post-graduate plans;

- eliminates administrative hurdles for students as they progress on their path to graduation;

- stays abreast of curricular changes in order to communicate key messages/deadlines, registration, financial aid, career support, and develops strategies for success both academic and otherwise;

- collaborates with faculty in all disciplines to stay on the cutting edge of industry standards and employer expectations in order to best coach new students;

- stays abreast of current and emerging trends which promote student success, including a strong awareness of the multitude of resources available at Maryville; and

- empowers students to develop and accomplish their personal, academic, and professional developmental goals.

With the implementation of the life-coaching model, underpinned by a centralized data platform and a collaborative mind-set embraced by the campus culture, freshman to sophomore retention rates have climbed to 88 percent and are still rising, and admission standards have not changed. Students are thriving at Maryville because learning and the support structures around that learning is personalized and focused.

Ultimately, personalized, holistic learning is a critical component to access and equity. It allows for a leveling of the playing field with a depth not yet seen at this magnitude in higher education, drastically increasing the chance of success for those for whom traditional learning methods have proven challenging or unsuccessful. All of this leads to the empowerment of individuals and communities toward a truly civil society. In the new university, we will bring data, brain research, learning theory, learning technology, cutting edge space design, and data-enriched advising and coaching to bear on the experience of our students and integrate it with the faculty's wealth of subject knowledge to design a personalized learning model for students. In this way, their success is not determined by how well they take or do not take a certain test, but rather their understanding and ability to apply what they learn to problem-solving and the real world. Such individualized and experiential instruction will take strong leadership, the right investments, new and evolving roles for faculty, and a radical refocusing on students as partners in learning. With greater depth of connection to individual learners, application numbers, retention, student success, graduation rates, and career outcomes all improve, resulting in a greater return on investment for each and every student.

The Student at the Center: Transforming Learning for the Future Challenge Questions

- Have you reviewed and improved your advising process in the last three years?

- Is your freshman to sophomore retention rate at or above the average for your Carnegie classification?

- Does your institution have a student success center?

- Does your institution provide assessment information to advisors of new students?

- Are there learning designers employed at your institution?

- Have you started a digital initiative at your institution?

- Do more than 50 percent of your professors teach in lecture format?

- Do your advisors do any vocational mentoring with students?

- Are your academic-affairs division and your student-affairs division integrated for student success?

- Do you have integrative experiences that carry your students from year one to year four?

- Do you have fully staffed career-development resources that can deliver services and support to students with a focus on vocational mentoring, internships, and job placement?

- Are outcomes for job placement above 80 percent at your institution?

- Do 100 percent of your students have an internship opportunity?

- Have you refreshed and revitalized your core curriculum in the last five years?

- When you are deciding on new academic programs, do you look at community and regional needs?

- Have you instituted professional development on current learning research for your faculty?

- Is all of the data that you have collected about individual students in one centralized data warehouse?

No Margin, No Mission: Running a University in the Black

Colleges and universities around the country are closing their doors. Layoffs, mergers, acquisitions, and multi-million-dollar budget deficits are bemoaned behind presidential closed doors and peppered across higher education news sources with alarming regularity. Public revelations of significant budget deficits deliver a blow to institutional self-esteem and block the ability to strategically move the organization forward. With sweeping budget cuts affecting everything from operations to student services, institutions convey a disjointed and inauthentic value proposition for students and families. While energy is being poured into navigating these financial crises, leaders neglect to keep a strong focus on their educational product and its relevance to the learner, leading to an inferior student experience and a long-term negative impact on the institution's viability.

We bear a responsibility to the families and students investing money in their hope for the future to steward their dollars with care. College and university leaders must explicitly, unequivocally embrace an entrepreneurial business mind-set, educating their campuses about the financial realities and complexities of institutional revenues, expenses, and discount rates. Without nurturing a level of financial health and sustainability that allows for strategic, ongoing reinvestment in the core of our work, institutional mission will not be achieved.

The vast majority of universities and colleges are designated as not-for-profits. Over the decades, that designation infused the culture of higher education in such a way that leadership often avoided basic business principles. If you talked about higher education as a business using terms like "margin," "customer," "market price," and so forth, the academy generally viewed you with disdain and suspicion, rejecting such terms as incompatible with education. In our careers, we have heard variations of the following statements hundreds of times from across the landscape:

- "Money will take the heart out of higher education forever."

- "This compromises the liberal arts."

- "A business demands autocratic management, and we have shared governance."

- "Decisions made for revenue reasons take away faculty academic freedom."

- "Money is not a motivator for us."

- "The programs that we offer should not be based on revenue."

- "Those high-demand programs that generate revenue cheapen the academic mission."

- "The term customer offends my soul!"

From the 1950s through 2000, insulated by the high demand for college degrees, higher education's disconnect from a business mind-set became so embedded that faculty and administrators became dismissive of concerns over the bottom line. As the baby boomer generation hit college age, the number of college students soared. Universities were able to raise tuition, fees, and other costs to align with their projected expenses without careful consideration for the rising cost of programs and personnel. Combined with a growing economic demand for a college-educated workforce, universities enjoyed more than a generation of growing enrollment. In this marketplace boom, there was little urgency about the bottom line (except, maybe, in the CFO's office).

Colleges and universities took on greater and greater debt to expand facilities and services and accommodate the expansive costs of running such a complex operation, inching tuition ever higher. Internally, the university-budget process became cripplingly complex. Faculty, administrators, and staff decided what they felt they needed and wanted for the next year. Through the collective input of these groups, cumbersome committees vetted hundreds of budget requests. If the current revenue level didn't support the scope of requests, many universities (certainly prior to the economic downturn of 2008–2010) raised tuition, annual fund goals, or new student enrollment goals to generate the dollars needed to fund the budget, without using appropriate historical trends or predictive modeling to determine whether meeting those goals was possible. In the vast majority of news articles regarding budget cuts at universities throughout the United

States, you will find a quote from an administrator stating some version of the following: "Our enrollment projections did not meet our budget allocations." In other words, we bet on something that didn't materialize. Shortfalls of this nature became commonplace.

As a result, tuition has increased well beyond inflation and cost of living for the average American family since 1980. According to Forbes, "Between 1985 and 2011, average tuition nationwide increased 498 percent—more than four times the rate of general inflation (114 percent) as measured by the Consumer Price Index (CPI)."[31] Institutional debt has risen to alarming levels. Colleges and universities collectively owe $240 billion, the Moody's bond-rating service reports. That debt rose 18 percent, to $145 billion, in the last five years at public universities, Moody's says. At privates, it went up 3 percent, to $95 billion.[32] As the dance between climbing debt and increasing tuition has continued, American demographics have shifted—the number of students graduating from high school will plateau, the middle class is shrinking, and a growing population of low socioeconomic students need additional support to afford the high cost of postsecondary education.[33] Discount rates are rising,

31 Lindsay, T. Tom Lindsay, "College Tuition Inflation: An Overblown Crisis?" Forbes, December 13, 2017, https://www.forbes.com/sites/tomlindsay/2017/12/13/college-tuition-inflation-an-overblown-crisis/#9d3ec82589e8.

32 Jon Marcus, "Like their students, colleges are vastly increasing the amount they borrow," The Hechinger Report , October 10, 2017, http://hechingerreport.org/like-their-students-colleges-are-vastly-increasing-the-amount-they-borrow/.

33 Rick Seltzer, "The High School Graduate Plateau," Inside Higher Ed, December 6, 2016, https://www.insidehighered.com/news/2016/12/06/high-school-graduates-drop-number-and-be-increasingly-diverse; "The American Middle Class is Losing Ground: No Longer the Majority and Falling Behind Financially," Pew Research Center, 2015, http://www.pewsocialtrends.org/2015/12/09/the-american-middle-class-is-losing-ground/; "The American Middle Class is Losing Ground: No Longer the Majority and Falling Behind Financially," Pew Research Center, (2015), http://www.pewsocialtrends.org/2015/12/09/the-american-middle-class-is-losing-ground/; Rana Forrhar, "The US College Debt Bubble

ultimately confusing the marketplace. The questions we hear so often from students and parents are, "How much do you really cost, and why do you cost so much?" A fiscal crisis with enormous impact on the viability of our marketplace is upon us.

Behind challenges to the cost of higher education lies the fundamental question of value—the relative worth, utility, or necessity—of the educational product. If students don't choose to attend our institutions, the core of the problem is with the value students perceive that they will get from the learning experience, not with institutional marketing or the admissions staff. If we choose to simply offset enrollment shortfalls with endowment funds or a push for increased giving, we ignore the underlying value proposition issue that must be solved. We live in a world where we charge money for an educational product, and our families have a choice of where to go. In this free-market business, we must constantly prove our value.

The key is always rethinking what we offer, the way we offer it, and the value proposition behind it. As a liberal arts university, if your enrollment is declining, ask yourself the following question: Are we delivering the liberal arts in a manner that is compelling to students? If the answer is that you are teaching them as you always have, then it's likely time to pivot. A critical part of every liberal arts institution's business strategy must be to make the relevance of the liberal arts clear and compelling. That is not the job of marketing and admissions, but the role and responsibility of leadership, vision, and strategic execution.

As the new university tackles its value proposition, it must also reexamine its core assumptions about budgeting and administer their finances like a business in order to create stability through good

is becoming dangerous," *Financial Times*, April 9, 2017, https://www.ft.com/content/a272ee4c-1b83-11e7-bcac-6d03d067f81f.

and bad times. First, we will examine two significant opportunities for business-minded pivotal change and growth in the future: the growth of partnerships between industry and education and managing cost and resource allocation across the academic unit. Second, we will explore a multifaceted construct for budgeting, from strategy around the role of leadership in the budget process to a recommended budgeting model and accompanying financial tactics, such as an examination of contingencies and endowment draws.

The Growth of Partnerships

One of the most significant ways in which we are watching institutions shift their business model is through a vast expansion in both the definition and depth of partnerships across their communities and regions. While much has changed since the publication of *Surviving to Thriving* five years ago, there remains a finite number of institutional revenue sources, reflected originally in that text.[34] Institutions can:

- **Grow:** Increase enrollment and retention.

- **Borrow:** Take on debt.

- **Shift:** Stop doing something in order to do something else.

- **Raise:** Work toward increased levels of constituent engagement around giving.

- **Alternate:** Explore alternative revenue streams.

- **Focus:** Find efficiencies in existing systems or programs in order to concentrate resources.

---

34   Joanne Soliday and Rick Mann, *Surviving to Thriving: A Planning Framework for Leaders of Private Colleges and Universities*, (Whitsett: Credo Press, 2013).

- **Partner:** Build interdependent relationships across the local and regional geography with mission-relevant foundations, businesses, and industries.

This seventh and final source of revenue has expanded by leaps and bounds even in the last five years. The ability of college trustees and leadership to identify significant partnerships that bring both capital and program money to the table around mission and strategic initiatives will be one of the key difference-makers in the health and sustainability of institutions into the future. There are a multitude of colleges and universities securing partnerships with local and regional foundations for geographically oriented initiatives from health care to ministry, and we are seeing strong, multipronged partnerships with significant corporations that nurture student connections from enrollment to job placement. For example, a university could find itself in a position to provide ongoing training and development for the employees of a regional corporation, and at the same time be forging a system for more internships and job placements at that same company. In the new university, the creative partnerships on the horizon are limited only by our ability to move with agility toward designing and implementing them.

Partnerships exist along a continuum that has expanded well beyond traditional cooperative-buying agreements. Among schools, those traditional forms of partnership are still utilized, resulting in operational cost savings such as cohort-organized representation. Between schools and businesses, simple cooperation provides placements for

> The creative partnerships on the horizon are limited only by our ability to move with agility toward designing and implementing them.

internships, clinical rotations, and general chamber-of-commerce alignments. However, in the new university, the institution is truly in co-creation mode with industry, government, higher-education associations, and other colleges and universities with the end goal of successfully addressing regional, state, and national needs. This level of strategic thinking moves partnerships well beyond a simple desire for survival or economies of scale into an emerging practice of coalitions for good.

DWU'S President Novak has always believed that linking hands with the region is vital to honoring the university's mission as well as to its growth and sustainability of both enrollment and philanthropic giving. Presidential time dedicated to regional relationships in South Dakota and the Great Plains has been instrumental to shifting the trajectory of DWU's future. The entrepreneurial heart of South Dakota's culture means that there is no budget at the state level for support of private higher education; private institutions are entirely self-funded. DWU's geographic reality also means that philanthropy frequently comes in the form of complex assets including land, timber, and cattle. As such, the success of the institution relies heavily on its connection to and deep understanding of the needs of the region. In 2013, President Novak convened a business-advisory group of fifty leaders representing seven industry sectors to examine how best to equip students for the future. Out of this emerged DWU's freshman course on innovation, problem-solving, and creativity, and a more intentional focus on soft-skills development across the general-education curriculum. With a greater understanding of DWU's goals and focus on the regional economy, business leaders were ready to invest in the institution, whose budget for capital improvement and new initiatives is now significantly enhanced by

THE CONTINUUM OF PARTNERSHIPS

Bluy Sky Ideas
- New Models
- Industry and Education
  Co-Creation

School & Business / Government
- Pipelines to Economic Development
- Solving Local and Regional
  Economic Problems

Business / Community
- Internships
- Financial Support
- Service and Leadership

Among Schools
- Procurement
- Representation
- Co-Curricular Programming

New levels of strategic thinking move partnerships well
beyond a simple desire for survival or economies of scale into
an emerging practice of creating coalitions for good.

partnership contributions that add value through dollars, human-resource investment, infrastructure investment, and advocacy.

Marian University offers another example of a traditional liberal arts institution opening its aperture in specific ways to balance the demands of mission with the needs of the marketplace to create a clear value proposition. They have placed the diversity of revenue streams at the front and center of their strategy. We've discussed their college of osteopathic medicine and its impact on the reimagining of existing programs and the development of new programs and initiatives; those revenue streams have been developed with deep connections to mission and vision. Marian understands that the needs of their region and their city will be a part of their economic and missional future. The hard work of the campus community to link with and leverage the assets of Indianapolis is at the forefront of conversation with almost anyone connected to the university. A refreshing look outward instead of inward has been at the core of financial strength and innovation. With simultaneous focus on both their unique value proposition and the need for increased revenue to invest in their mission, Marian has created an explicit, financially viable business foundation on which they examine expansion and the evolution of their work.

Bigger Than Efficiency: Managing Cost Across the Academic Unit

Student learning is our enterprise; it's why our institutions exist. The heart of our business is the development and execution of learning that results in transformed students who are prepared for and confident about their contribution to society and their ability to secure a meaningful life. With that student transformation at the center of institutional investment, cost across the academic unit must be closely examined, and university leaders must be ready to evaluate, limit, or eliminate any academic program if the numbers, trends, and projections are not satisfactory for the expense to the institution. But when we approach that enterprise with efficiency as the only measure, we risk the demise of quality. Instead, our colleague Dr. Joretta Nelson strongly recommends that any discussion about costs are driven by:

- an agreed-upon definitions of program excellence,

- a robust publicly available data, and

- a practice of allocating resources based on demonstrated quality.

Within that environment, the dependent variable is not just net revenue per full-time enrolled student, but more importantly, the quality of student-learning outcomes. That environment drives innovative and experimental thinking rather than protectionism and fear. There are three levels of work that should be taking place at all times related to academic efficiencies:

Level One: Operational

An operational-level approach analyzes distributions of both time and space with an end-goal of maximizing class sizes, frequency of offerings, and faculty deployment. This first stage of analysis typically generates substantive resource savings as academic administration recognizes the costs of multiples course sections, poorly designed course rotations, costly faculty release time inequities, and unbalanced advising loads. This is also the level for classroom-utilization analyses; spaces not fully utilized at maximum capacity or time-schedule can create the illusion that additional space must be built or rented when instead, adjustment of schedule and

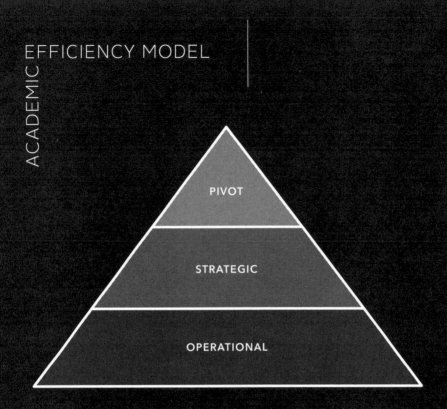

ACADEMIC EFFICIENCY MODEL

PIVOT
Learning Questions:
a. Flexible delivery modalities
b. Comprehensive competencies
c. Pathways through and beyond
d. Thriving pathways for all students

STRATEGIC
Program Considerations:
- Program Cost Analysis
- Program Value Assessment Model
- New Program Development & Launch Model

OPERATIONAL
Academic Operational and Environmental Efficiencies:
- Classroom & Space Utilization
- Class Size
- Faculty Deployment
- Release Time
- Advising Loads

release of building or classroom "ownership" is required: i.e., creating departmental willingness to share spaces across disciplines.

Level Two: Strategic

A strategic-level approach represents both the analysis of program costs but more importantly, the rubrics for program development. At this stage, the institution comes to agreement on how programs will be valued. This process of determining which variables will be utilized, and how they will be weighted, is most effectively implemented if developed collaboratively between administration and faculty. Many institutions focus only on academic programs in this level and miss the opportunity to look at all learning programs on campus. This means including advising, academic support, high-impact practices, and all components of the co-curricular experience. While existing programs are the initial focus, the true value in adopting this practice is in how new programs are evaluated and launched.

Level Three: Pivot

This the highest stage of academic strategic thinking where larger learning questions are considered, such as:

- What is the value of the common core?

- Why do students need this particular number of credit hours to graduate?

- What benefits might we see from increasing transferability of credits between institutions?

- What would it look like if we added co-curricular portfolios that reflected deeper layers of learning?

- What hybrid modalities would allow for shortened time to degree?

If the goal is continued development of margin for the sake of mission, the existing models of educational delivery must evolve. Efficiency must be an outcome of innovative, effective learning experiences.

Spelman offers us an example of an institution where ongoing focus on managing cost across the academic unit, in constant connection to mission and vision, has reaped great success. While other colleges are suffering from years of accumulating majors and programs that now need to be evaluated and cut, Spelman has been lean by design. There are only twenty-seven majors: the number was simply never allowed to increase. The top three majors at the college are psychology, biology, and political science, and Spelman has placed specific intentionality around resourcing these critical pipelines. As a result, Spelman awards more degrees to Black women in STEM than any other institution in the country. At a time where the attrition rate in STEM is 48 percent by the sophomore year for all students nationwide—and Black women are one of the most vulnerable populations for attrition in this area—Spelman has increased the number of STEM majors by 12 percent by the sophomore year over a period of two years. Spelman is the largest producer of Black women scientists in the world and continues to be the most successful pipeline for the growth of that number. Being intentionally efficient has allowed them to concentrate on the diverse ways that students learn, instead of the "right-sizing" of offerings that is now necessary across the nation.

DWU also addressed academic costs early in its pivot, repositioning its ability to invest in its core mission through the elimination of six majors, the closing of a satellite campus, and the elimination of an ancillary enterprise, a day care. The university experienced subsequent savings from this process, which were invested in new strategic initiatives including support for experiential learning, expansion of their strengths-based Learn Strong program, revisions to the core curriculum, new online-program offerings, and targeted expansion of junior varsity programs in athletics. Every year there is a thorough scan of programs succeeding and those that are not. When growth potential is clear, a program is given additional resources to expand. Other programs are eliminated. Each department budget at the institution must be defended yearly, and new and innovative initiatives are encouraged. With a commitment to operate in the leanest way, DWU is positioned to fund more and more pilot projects to test their relevance and grow their success.

Tackling the Budget

Central to the new university's business model must be a strategically focused, reimagined budgeting process that begins and ends with leadership. The process should clearly reflect the mandate that fiduciary authority rests solely with the board of trustees, which vests that power in the president. Nearly every set of bylaws state this in some fashion, and legal counsel will tell the board that this is the case in the eyes of the law. Faculty, staff, departments, and divisions can and should articulate what they think they need and how it relates to the mission, vision, and strategic plan for the university. But decision-making authority for where funds are allocated and spent must rest with the president, chief financial officer, and the senior leadership they choose to involve. Further, the finance committee of the board can and should exercise its role to oversee the president at a broad, strategic level in those decisions.

The new university will have a finance team composed of the board committee, president, CFO, and senior staff educated around a clear understanding of the realities of strong business practices, with a clear set of priorities about how budgets are constructed and managed, as well as a centralized budget-management and planning process.

Budget planning is like a Rubik's cube. Each decision or move impacts all the others, and each expenditure must be made at the right time in the right order to maximize the positive impact on students and student learning. Put another way, there may be ten worthwhile budget-expenditure ideas, but the order in which you initiate them can minimize or maximize their positive impact. Only senior leadership connected to the institution's strategic framework and examining budget inputs in the aggregate are qualified to make those judgements. Abandoning the notion of consensus (as discussed in the "Courageous Leadership" chapter) is critical to the success of the budgeting process in the new university. Budget planning and decision-making is a complex process and set of calculations that cannot be hostage to something as amorphous as consensus. Striving for accord will insure stasis, fiscal mistakes, and a failure to invest in priorities and capitalize on important opportunities.

Embracing a Zero-Based Budgeting Philosophy

In order for leadership to most appropriately weigh the funding of strategic initiatives and all other budget inputs, the institutional budget should be built each year on a zero-based budget philosophy, with focus on a "repeatable process ... to rigorously review every dollar in the annual budget, manage financial performance on a monthly basis, and build a culture of cost management among all employees."[35] In the institutional context, a zero-based budget starts with the strategic plan and mission of the university and identifies its core elements. Once those elements are funded and layered appropriately, then all other items can be added that are essential to student learning and operational success. With a focus on creating a culture of accountability and intentionality around expenses, each department and division is asked to rebuild its budget from the ground up and justify line item inclusions annually. That which does not fit is eliminated, modified in scope, or held in abeyance until enrollment numbers are solidified. A zero-based approach provides the discipline to carefully consider first what is truly necessary to accomplish the mission and strategy. This careful consideration means the budget process for each year is longer, starts earlier, and must be based on solid data analytics regarding revenue generated, expenses, future trends, and a clear understanding of the priorities of the institution.

In Maryville's case, the board and the leadership were serious about bringing clarity, focus, and attention to the financial life of the institution, while they continued to keep students at the center of their focus. When clear financial accountability and agile decision-making around zero-based budgeting were integrated into the culture, surpluses became normal. Vice President for Finance Steve Mandeville says, "Our budgeting process starts with the strategic plan. We look at what each goal and objective will cost, and we divide the budget accordingly. Then we look carefully at what we are contractually obligated for. We revisit things each year to be sure they are still relevant and valuable, and we give funding first to the

---

35   Sean Callahan, Kyle Hawke, and Carey Mignerey, "Five Myths and Realities about Zero-Based Budgeting," McKinsey and Company, October 2014, https://www. mckinsey.com/business-functions/strategy-and-corporate-finance/our-insights/ five-myths-and-realities-about-zero-based-budgeting.

identified priorities in the strategic plan. It's important for budgeting to be an educative process so the campus community understands why surpluses are so important for the growth of the institution and required in order to provide better service to our students." How many strategic priorities have gone unfunded at institutions across the country because leaders have lacked the courage to stop doing something that is no longer relevant or critical? At Maryville, aligning funding with strategic initiatives and working toward the greatest return on those investments has been critical to success.

Many universities are experts at adding onto the budget, but not at reorienting priorities year-to-year. For example, if it is determined in the strategic plan that tablet technology in the classrooms and new learning spaces are essential, then money must be earmarked to accomplish that goal first. Essentially, we can't agree something is a priority and then try to find the money as an add-on to everything else. If everything is a priority, then nothing is a priority. Zero-based budgeting is critical because it forces everyone to assess value continuously, not just once. It forces all members of the campus community, over time, to tie everything to the strategic plan, and ultimately to investment in students and their learning first.

> If everything is a priority, then nothing is a priority.

People and Technology: A New Balance

As learning changes, so too does the financial approach to every college and university's largest investment: people and labor. The new university will examine its labor force with the following assumption: the effectiveness and efficiency of the teams and systems that directly impact student learning, service, and success are critically important. All other functions that are indirectly related must be planned for outsourcing or automation as technology can facilitate. At most universities, private or public, labor costs run as high as 70 to 80 percent of the overall budget.[36] We see time and time again that the first request in any budget meeting is typically for more faculty and staff to deliver the work of their department or division. In the current landscape, efforts should be made to evaluate all of those requests in light of what is becoming technologically possible.

In our digital world, student service—or any service, for that matter—does not necessarily mean human contact. If students are able do all of their banking or product purchasing online, they should also be able to do many university transactions online with the convenience of their smart phone. Dependency on location and human interaction for all services is counterintuitive. The best service is that which provides the greatest access and simplest interface—which, increasingly, is not inherently tied to human interaction but instead to automation or artificial intelligence, likely the most rapidly developing and impactful area of technological change for colleges and universities to lean into. Properly adopted and applied, artificial intelligence can replace a number of existing support functions in the academy, allowing for an appropriately reduced dependency on support labor. Roles that can be automated or supported by artificial intelligence should be eliminated in order to lower costs and maintain the central role of faculty, coaches, and support staff with direct-contact roles with students.

---

36   Donna M. Desrochers and Rita Kirshstein, "Labor Intensive or Labor Expensive? Changing Staffing and Compensation Patterns in Higher Education," February 2014, https://www.air.org/sites/default/files/downloads/report/DeltaCostAIR-Labor-Expensive-Higher-Education-Staffing-Brief-Feb2014.pdf.

This leads to the fact that a foundational dimension of the business model of the new university is a priority investment in connectivity. The learning society of today demands connectivity. It is the lifeblood of access to content, and that is the fundamental precept of learning. The new university will invest the necessary resources in wireless and wired networks that make the entire campus, indoors and out, a learning space. This facilitates classrooms without walls, problem-solving group work, student research, and study. In other words, connectivity is the new library of the twenty-first century. Universities must make a serious and profound commitment to wireless connectivity, speed, and bandwidth. A university can expect to spend roughly $1,000 per institutional FTE (students, faculty, and staff) on information-technology services. A private non-research university with five thousand students and a corresponding average fifteen hundred employees can therefore expect to spend $6.5 million in its capital IT budget.[37] That is not computer replacement and printers, but infrastructure and connectivity. Constant learning is as reliant on connectivity as society is reliant on electricity—without it, we cannot effectively compete for the digital natives for whom connectivity is an integral component of a valuable experience. Connectivity leads to the delivery of more efficient services, information, and ultimately education, and it is the space where our customer, i.e. student, lives today—digitally.

The Endowment Controversy

The role of the endowment, long the holy grail of fiscal success and stability, must be questioned as we reimagine the institutional

---

37   Leah Lang, "2016 EDUCAUSE Core Data Service (CDS) Benchmarking Report," EDUCAUSE, April 11, 2017, https://library.educause.edu/resources/2017/4/2016-educause-core-data-service-cds-benchmarking-report.

business model. Endowments have long been an important financial tool used by institutions to defray student costs through scholarships, which is a healthy and positive use. Endowment draws that support increasing access at an institution are vital and laudable, but two unfortunate scenarios emerge:

1. Often, the endowment is used to fund operational budgets. Whether this is a planned annual draw to reduce dependency on tuition revenue from enrollment or it is a reaction to immediate or ongoing revenue shortfalls, relying on the endowment for operational funds is a dangerous narcotic. If revenue projection is not realistic and owned by those responsible for the activities driving revenues, then the endowment draw simply enhances a university's ability to add more requests to the pie, leading to complacency.

2. Universities often place inordinate focus on growing the endowment instead of raising both unrestricted and restricted dollars to directly fund strategic initiatives. We must recognize that we will not be able to effectively pivot if we are raising endowment numbers when there is not enough money to appropriately invest in strategies that will be transformative to net revenue and institutional mission.

The Importance of Contingencies

To hedge against the inevitable unexpected, during the budgeting process universities should focus on a foundation of contingency funds that can be built in and across the budget for a controlled amount of flexibility across available dollars. Every university should work toward a top-line budget contingency of 2.5 to 3.5 percent of the overall budget that is untouchable except in the case of emergencies, and wherever possible, build in smaller contingencies across individual line items. Depending on the size of a university budget, these smaller contingencies can ideally grow to several hundred thousand dollars and can, if necessary, become available to offset costs for key strategic goals where needed. However, contingencies should never be spent in full in any given year. Ideally, at least 60 to 80 percent (100 percent, if possible) should be saved so that the university can build up a cash reserve separate from the endowment. Preparing appropriately for a shortfall or fiscal crisis means applying the discipline to underestimate your revenue and overestimate your expenses. In this way, universities can ensure, at the very least, fiscal stability, and in some years, modest to moderate growth in cash reserves.

If institutions do not attack a pivot in their business model with vigor, they will either cut themselves to the bone while offering an increasingly irrelevant product to their students, or they will fail and close. There is one central question that must be asked and answered in every budget decision: how does this allocation benefit our students? If the answer isn't clear, direct, and connected, then the budget request cannot be a priority. It does not mean that particular investment is inherently wrong, it just means it won't come first. If the budget, investments, and revenue projections are conservative and grounded in sound business principles, universities can and will produce revenue. They must do so in order to invest appropriately in a high-quality experience inside and outside the classroom that results in the desired student outcomes.

No Margin, No Mission: Running a University in the Black Challenge Questions

- Are strategic initiatives funded before anything else in the budgeting process?

- Do you annually set aside money for contingencies in your budget?

- Are your faculty and staff fully informed and knowledgeable about your budgeting process?

- Do your faculty and staff have institutional financial literacy?

- Have you had a budget surplus in the last three years?

- Is surplus in the budget reinvested strategically in mission-centered initiatives?

- In a budget deficit, are adjustments made that create efficiencies in the organization rather than impact to learning?

- Is each department or division at your institution asked to rebuild and justify its budgets annually?

- Have you taken a close look at academic efficiencies in the last three years?

- Are clear business plans developed to inform decisions about new programs and initiatives?

- Is financial modeling used when examining the viability of a new program?

- Is there an efficient and effective process for eliminating programs that don't meet original goal measures?

- Does your institution have a discount rate for traditional students of over 50 percent?

- Do you currently have a revenue stream based on adult students over twenty-three years old?

- Is your traditional student enrollment growing?

- Is your non-traditional student enrollment growing?

- Are your retention and graduation percentages increasing?

- As a central piece of financial sustainability, is your value proposition distinctive and clear?

- Do you have five or more working partnerships with regional or national funders that impact your margin?

- Have you taken the steps to be an attractive and flexible partner?

- Have you drawn funds from your endowment at a rate of over 5 percent in the last three years?

- Do you use endowment funds for anything other than scholarship aid?

The Explosion of Adult Education: Meeting Society's Needs

Almost thirty million working adults in the United States aspire to complete a college degree they began years ago, and more than forty million others could enhance their career prospects, but have never attended a higher-education institution.[38] These tens of millions of people want to go back to college to pursue their dreams and often become mired in bureaucratic barriers such as transfer credit obstacles; scheduling conflicts; distance to the nearest college, university, or satellite campus; the need for letters of reference and test scores from decades earlier; and a prohibitive cost structure. At a time when we urgently need a growing, skilled workforce to assume

---

38   "A Stronger Nation: Learning beyond high school builds American talent," Lumina Foundation, accessed October 15, 2018, http://strongernation. luminafoundation.org/report/2018/#nation.

the jobs of today and tomorrow, we are putting multiple obstacles in the path of precisely the people who can fill those needs.

The reality is that we must continue to look beyond traditional-age education into more diverse markets and revenue streams where education is most needed. If higher-education institutions of all sizes and types ignore the emerging adult market within their region or beyond, they tie one arm behind their backs in terms of relevant learning, revenue streams, and balanced fiscal portfolios. Innovative programs for adult learners that connect our mission in higher education to a demonstrated need in our communities and our world will play a critical role in securing the sustainability and relevance of higher education into the future.

Historically, colleges and universities have focused primarily on youth as the common denominator for worthiness to pursue a college education. It has only been in the last thirty to fifty years that the concept of education for working adults has entered the landscape.[39] In the postwar era, and particularly in the 1970s and 1980s, the economic evolution in many western societies (from manufacturing age to an information age) drove working adults into an "education-for-advancement" mode.[40] Increasingly, education was seen as a way for working adults to expand on skills needed in their current jobs, perhaps start a new career, and ultimately change their lives. As a result, many universities across the country introduced the first generation of adult education and built it around the convenience of nights, weekends, and condensed formats designed to

39 "Changes in the American workplace," Pew Research Center, October 6, 2016, http://www.pewsocialtrends.org/2016/10/06/1-changes-in-the-american-workplace/.

40 Ali Berker, Lena Horn, and C. Dennis Carroll, "Work First, Study Second: Adult Undergraduates Who Combine Employment and Postsecondary Enrollment," U.S. Department of Education, Institute of Education Sciences, 2003, https://nces.ed.gov/pubs2003/2003167.pdf.

meet the lifestyle demands of adults and their families. This opening of the campus to after-hours instruction was a service, a convenience for working adults, and it led to an explosion in the adult-education field.[41] From that time until now, we have also seen the nature of work and the geography of the workplace change. Skills that were never needed ten years ago are now in high demand. Training and skill development, which was once done in face-to-face formats, is now largely delivered through technology. We are truly becoming a culture dependent upon lifelong learning.

The original successes in this market were voluminous. Many universities built significant enrollment by catering to adult learners. Yet while some embraced this growing need, just as many universities decided to eschew this market for a variety of reasons. Adult learners' qualifications often rest heavily in their work and life experience, and university leadership struggled to align this with deeply ingrained notions of admissions requirements and the selectivity rankings connected to them. Administration and faculty also believed they could not recreate their core learning experience for a different population and appropriately connect it to their mission in the same way for adult students. Additionally, education for working adults meant faculty teaching on nights and weekends, and many wished to maintain traditional hours and flexibility rather than the hours that would be of more convenience to these learners.

More importantly, over the decades we have erected a series of false barriers between education and skill development. The reality is that these elements are two sides of the same coin. Students of all ages and backgrounds need to be taught critical thinking,

---

41   Louis Soares, "Post-traditional Learners and the Transformation of Postsecondary Education: A Manifesto for College Leaders," American Council on Education, January 2013, https://www.acenet.edu/news-room/Documents/Post-Traditional-Learners.pdf.

communication, writing, and problem-solving, and they also need and demand skills and abilities specific to particular professions. All individuals who graduate from college today are going to encounter the need for more education, more training, and more skill development during their professional lives. Consider the sobering demographic and economic realities in this century that directly impact the world of higher education. As many as 30 percent of workers will lose their current jobs due to automation as their jobs are replaced by some form of artificial intelligence. McKinsey and company provide a thorough, global view on the impact of AI and automation.[42] For example, when driverless cars become the norm, some four million people who make a living as drivers will be out of work and will need new careers. Estimates around the impact of driverless automobiles range from a few million to as many as eleven million.[43] In the field of banking, local branches with tellers, bank managers, and loan officers will dwindle as perhaps 50 percent of banking needs will be handled online, facilitated by artificial intelligence. Banking too is an oft discussed industry of higher paid workers who could be impacted by AI.[44] If these statistics are not sobering enough, recent predictions by experts studying the advancement of human and machine partnerships estimate that

---

42   James Manyika et al., "Jobs Lost, Jobs Gained: Workforce transitions in a time of automation," McKinsey Global Institute, McKinsey & Company, 2017, https://www.mckinsey.com/featured-insights/future-of-organizations-and-work/Jobs-lost-jobs-gained-what-the-future-of-work-will-mean-for-jobs-skills-and-wages.

43   Stick Shift: Autonomous Vehicles, Driving Jobs, and the Future of Work, (Washington, DC: Center for Global Policy Solutions, 2017); Ben Leubsdorf, "Self-Driving Cars Could Transform Jobs Held by 1 in 9 U.S. Workers," Wall Street Journal, (August 14, 2017),https://blogs.wsj.com/economics/2017/08/14/self-driving-cars-could-transform-jobs-held-by-1-in-9-u-s-workers/.

44   Kevin Smith, "Artificial intelligence will wipe out half the banking jobs in a decade, experts say," Chicago Tribune, April 23, 2018, www.chicagotribune.com/business/ct-biz-artificial-intelligence-bank-jobs-20180423-story.html.

85 percent of jobs in which today's learners will be engaged in 2030 have not been invented yet. The emergence of new careers as the positive side of this economic upheaval is discussed in depth in many locations, including the Institute for the Future's report predicting 85 percent of new careers [45] There will be hundreds of thousands of workers seeking to enter these new and challenging careers, and they will need an education to do it.

Over the next decade, we will see that badges, certificates, microdegrees, traditional undergraduate degrees, and a growing variation of graduate degrees will be available and delivered to learners of all ages by the institutions that are innovative and nimble enough to do so quickly and with flexibility. Non-traditional students have varied backgrounds and experiences, and bring passion, dedication, and abilities that can be transformative to an institution. We believe it is a great loss for independent colleges and universities and their student-centered missions not to embrace this enormous niche wholeheartedly, with programs, policies, and procedures that address and support their needs. There has never been another time in history when there was a greater need for adults to have access to deeper thinking, training, and skill development, most accurately termed continuous career education. In the new university, continuous career education must:

1. **Focus on asking the questions "What?" and "Why?"** in order to maintain a strong connection to mission and vision while still being responsive to market needs.

---

45   "The Next Era of Human | Machine Partnerships: New Report Explores Emerging Technologies' Impact on Society & Work in 2030," Institute for the Future, July 12, 2017, http://www.iftf.org/humanmachinepartnerships/.

2. **Have the agility to meet the needs of emerging careers**
    with relevant programs, partnering with industry and
    learning designers for rich, rapid curriculum development.

3. **Offer the appropriate modality and companion
    services** that address the convenience, flexibility, and
    connection necessary for this population to see the hope in
    completing the next phase of their learning.

1. Maintaining Connection to Mission and Vision

For the leadership at most institutions, one of the first questions
that must be answered when considering continuous career
education is: How can we step into this marketplace with distinction
and relevance? This is a space in which independent colleges and
universities have an opportunity to set themselves apart from large
public institutions and community colleges. The transformational
nature of a liberal arts education can be applied in relevant,
connected ways to adult learners if institutions undertake programs
that represent a strong reflection of institutional identity. We must
ask ourselves: What unique space do we fill in the marketplace that
could translate effectively to a different student population?

For some, that space may be embedded in a professional or
entrepreneurial spirit. For others, like DWU, development in this area
is carefully aligned toward the needs of the region and connected to
the institutional vision of being an incubator for economic growth.
One new program that honors DWU's Methodist faith will connect
with rural pastors through a unique lens: DWU will not offer
theological education for pastors but will instead address leadership
models that allow those pastors to be more effective in their
communities, preparing them for issues surrounding stewardship,

talent-asset management, and running a strong church-based operation. Additionally, DWU will launch a program to certify trust-management professionals. South Dakota holds nearly $200 billion in trust assets and there are only two other programs in the country equipping learners for work in this growth area. The development of a robust LPN-BS program in nursing further responds to regional demands in the health care workforce. In these programs, DWU is not attempting to reach national audiences. Their goal is to pilot programs that impact those in their communities, review and assess them carefully, and then decide whether they can be helpful to the nation or the world.

2. Agility, Relevance, and Learning Design

Curriculum development must use speed-to-market as a key success measure. The new university cannot spend two years thinking about a program and another year developing it for delivery. In the new university, the addition of new programs is an administrative, business-oriented decision. Market analysis of emerging careers and needs must become an ongoing focus, either through investment in a highly-developed office of institutional research or by a strong relationship with an external research partner. This research will be used strategically and quickly to determine which programs should be introduced based on market demand before bringing together a structured group of faculty members to engage in their development and launch.

We have seen great success achieved in the areas of program development and curriculum design when an institution can begin with a coalition of the willing—those faculty and staff who understand the landscape of adult learning and are philosophically convinced of the need. No faculty member should be forced to engage in this kind of innovative and agile work, but neither should those who stand in opposition be allowed to block progress in this important space. It is possible to find those faculty and staff members, in every institution, who are ready and willing to take a step in this direction—begin with them. If there is not a willingness in any sector of the institution to begin, then new voices may need to be hired. As with so many changes, culture is key. Structures around rewarding innovation in this area, along with proven successes both in student learning and increased institutional revenue, can go a long way toward creating buy-in across the institution for this work.

Universities must then blast open the doors to curriculum design. They must bring industry professionals and practitioners into the room to fashion curriculum together, as a team, so that the instruction and content will provide the education that meets employer needs. The curriculum will be flexible and adjustable as those skills and abilities change, and the success of that partnership with industry will be measured by the employability and career outcomes of its graduates. Creatively designed curriculum can achieve both education consistent with the liberal arts *and* the need for profession-specific skills. In fact, the attention to learning design for online courses can and should push classroom professors to see their course syllabi in different ways. The structure of project work and facilitation of information by online instructors offers rich learning for all of us who spend most of our time in traditional classrooms.

Maryville University's Active Learning Ecosystem (A.L.E.) offers an example of intentional learning design. With the A.L.E.'s focus on individualized learning, necessary emphasis has been placed on innovative and experiential teaching that capitalizes on the information available to instructors about their students. In addition to Maryville's online programs providing a healthy revenue stream with which to reinvest in the core institutional mission, you'll find as much passion for quality and the success of students here as you do in the traditional undergraduate experience.

Maryville owes much of its success in this area to strong academic leadership that took an institutional vision and poured it into and across the academic unit. The recently-retired academic leader at Maryville was a long-standing cabinet member with an extraordinary passion for excellence in teaching and learning. Former Vice President of Academic Affairs Dr. Mary Ellen Finch served as Maryville's academic leader for ten years and as dean of the school of education and in various other roles for another thirty-four years. Her stability brought trust and wisdom to the vision. We make special note of Dr. Finch because the masterful skill of advocating for faculty and mobilizing change is essential to every college or university wanting to make a pivot, and Dr. Finch possessed this skill in spades. Without academic leaders who embrace agility and innovation, turning institutional ships toward the future of learning will be impossible.

In the Finch Center for Teaching and Learning at Maryville, every faculty member has access to curriculum-design specialists who serve as partners to faculty as they bring their learning content to the table. The learning team of faculty member and design specialist works in tandem to integrate experiences, technology, and group projects that will engage students and improve learning outcomes. The partnership is available for online and classroom learning and has begun to permeate the entire culture of teaching and learning at the university. There is a synergy that emerges when a faculty member sees that the value of content can be increased dramatically with learning design. Content centered in experiential teaching and the use of available technology is a stimulating incentive to learn by solving relevant real-world problems. Some critical aspects of the learning designer's role are:

- Working with subject matter experts, course developers, and adult and online education staff to design and develop online and blended courses.

- Providing technical and pedagogical assistance to faculty in the design, development, and implementation of online and blended courses.

- Writing, editing, designing, and creating online learning modules.

- Providing input to faculty on technical and instructional design aspects of developing blended and online learning applications.

- Researching and recommending appropriate media and methods for learning and designing learning programs using appropriate methods.

- Participating in the course evaluation/assessment process to determine course effectiveness.

3. Convenience, Flexibility, and Connection

The need for working adults to balance job responsibilities, childcare, eldercare, and all the other myriad roles they must play demands a delivery modality for their education that meets them in their own time and space. A new generation of online learning that utilizes the best of technology and learning design is opening doors for more and more institutions and learners to come together in effective, innovative teaching and learning—a far cry from the early days of online programs. When online education began twenty-five years ago, it was rudimentary, static, and broadly a passive exercise of watching traditionally produced lecture content disseminated on a computer screen. This first generation of online education was pushed forward by mostly for-profit schools in a low-quality manner with what we know now as predatory pricing. As a result, it received a deservedly bad reputation. In subsequent years, online learning has undergone a fundamental and dynamic rebirth. The delivery system has evolved to include greater and more robust content, expanded interactive experiences, and greater faculty-student engagement. It also has been adopted by respected public and private universities that honed the tools to make quality the key component.

Now in its third generation of development, online education is the newest area of innovation in the educational marketplace. With rich virtual learning environments, concept-mastery-based progression through learning, and a focus on both project-based and collaborative learning, the online space has, in some cases, been able to adopt impactful, research-based learning practices more effectively and quickly than a traditional classroom environment. Many universities provide online instruction developed by faculty and assisted by learning designers who are skilled in the technological presentation of the content. But even today, research shows that there is a marked generational bias around online instruction. The baby boomer generation views online learning as inferior, easier, weak, and lacking rigor when compared to classroom instruction, largely because they remember those first, rudimentary forays into online instruction and because it is difficult for them to imagine learning without a close personal relationship with a faculty member. Millennials and Gen X-ers view online instruction favorably, as a natural outgrowth of the technological age and often a preferred form of learning.[46] More than 30 percent of all graduating high school students will have some form of online learning before they graduate, and that number is increasing annually.[47]

Online delivery is sophisticated in breaking down the boundaries of access. It can be tailored and structured to meet different learning styles and approaches in ways that in-class instruction cannot. Online education also reaches students where they are, physically and academically, so that their education can fill a critical need as well as enrich their local communities. Two examples come to mind:

1. **Rural nurses:** The need for doctors and nurse practitioners in rural areas is extreme. Online instruction allows nurses in rural areas to receive the continuing education they need and to be able to apply it in their own communities, thus allowing them to remain in those communities and develop professionally. Health care partnerships like this, as well as with other critical industries and economic drivers, will help us grow the quality of employees in the workplace and the quality of the services provided to us all. These types of relationships also open doors to other dimensions of both non-profit and for-profit partnerships that help grow our colleges and universities.

2. **Coding:** There are over half a million open coding jobs in the United States and less than sixty thousand annual

---

46 John J.Matt, Frances L. O'Reilly, and Chad J. Williams, "Generational Perspective of Higher Educational Online Student Learning Styles," Journal of Education and Learning, May 2014, https://files.eric.ed.gov/fulltext/EJ1076418.pdf.

47 Julia E. Seaman, I. Elaine Allen, and Jeff Seaman, "Grade Increase: Tracking Distance Education in the United States," Babson Survey Research Group, http://onlinelearningsurvey.com/reports/gradeincrease.pdf.

graduates to fill them.[48] There is an extraordinary need for coding as a discipline, skill, and area of instruction to be developed in partnership with industry and delivered in such a way that those jobs can be filled by people within the communities where the jobs exist. These roles bring with them salary and benefits that can change people's lives.

In addition, the online format allows universities to tap into teaching talent across the country and beyond from expert scholars and practitioners. It also allows universities to avoid high overhead costs and satellite campus facilities that drain funds and drive up expenses for the student-consumer. This evolution of the online experience also will be important over the next decades to eliminate the prejudice around adjunct professor status and embrace an "experienced practitioner" label for those who are capable and willing to be a part of this movement toward wider access to learning, broadening and diversifying the lens of instruction to be welcoming and inclusive of both seasoned professors and practical professionals.[49]

In light of this need, Maryville has expanded their faculty structure to better reflect a heterogeneity of faculty talent, practitioner engagement, and adjunct retention and importance. Maryville hires faculty into tenure-track positions in key areas, but

---

48   Sarah Kessler, "You Probably Should Have Majored in Computer Science," Quartz, March 10, 2017, https://qz.com/929275/you-probably-should-have-majored-in-computer-science/.

49   The growing use of adjuncts has many causes and many impacts. The important notation here is that online education gives students access to professionals who do not want full teaching loads but whose knowledge and expertise can be decidedly beneficial to student learning.

they also now hire faculty into two levels of instructors to address key needs within and beyond online programs:

1. The first-level instructors teach a three/three load (while full-time faculty teach a normal four/four load) with no advising or committee responsibilities and receive full medical benefits. Their contract terms are for two years and are renewable based on enrollment needs.

2. The second-level instructors teach a five/five load without committee or advising responsibilities, with full medical benefits, and a salary at the higher-education-industry market rate for the discipline. These contracts are also two-year renewable and have the potential to be converted to tenure track when enrollment demands and performance warrant.

This multi-layered approach allows for a more nuanced approach to faculty recruitment and retention, satisfies the growing need for strong instruction that can fluctuate with changing enrollment patterns in disciplines, and brings a variety of perspectives into student learning.

If colleges and universities do not provide education and skill development for this exploding population of continuous learners, someone else will. Corporations like Google, Amazon, Apple, and start-ups like Coursera will—and are already beginning to—fill the void if universities fail to adapt pedagogy and delivery to meet this growing demand.[50] If institutions exhibit nimbleness and creativity in the development and launch of such programs as workforce

---

50   Doug Lederman, "Amazon Snags a Higher Ed Superstar," Inside Higher Ed, January 29, 2018, https://www.insidehighered.com/digital-learning/article/2018/01/29/amazons-high-profile-hire-higher-education-candace-thille.

needs change, corporations and businesses will look to partner with higher education to retrain their workforce around new skill sets and the technologies that accompany them. If we do not embrace this delivery system and the philosophical approach it demands, we will not be able to make education "Amazon-proof."

In the new university of the twenty-first century, continuous career education will be part of the ongoing relationship that higher-education institutions have with their undergraduates and alumni and a way to create a profoundly positive impact on their communities. We are beginning to see movement toward offering online classes to traditional students to fulfill prerequisite requirements and make more rapid progress toward graduate degrees. When introduced early and connected to the undergraduate experience, online courses and continuous education can become a powerful vehicle through which institutions deepen connections to their alumni, strengthening engagement and commitment over a much longer period of time. Helping working adults gain the education and skills they need to move into growing, thriving fields can mean corporate investment in learning partnerships, community empowerment, and regional economic development—ultimately elevating the community and our nation as a whole.

Universities must ask themselves some simple but profound questions about mission. Why wouldn't they want to provide life-long learning opportunities to their alumni? Why wouldn't they want to help build a more skilled workforce and create economic opportunity in their communities? Why wouldn't they want to provide an opportunity to those whose career paths must shift in a rapidly changing global economic landscape? The answer is simple: no school committed to education and empowerment should turn their back on this population and its growing education needs. The new university must embrace continuous career education to best serve our world.

The Explosion of Adult Education: Meeting Society's Needs Challenge Questions

- Does your institution feel a responsibility to educate learners of any age?

- Are there barriers to the education of adults at your institution?

- Are there barriers to online education at your institution?

- Do you believe that adult students must have the same experience as traditional students in order to secure a degree at your institution?

- Is your institution positioned to be able to move at the speed that the learning marketplace demands, and will demand into the future?

- Can your institution embrace the experience of professionals in specific fields as credentialed deliverers of online education?

- Do you believe you have a responsibility to your community and to your region in the area of continuous career development?

- Does your institution believe there is a role for online education in the traditional student curriculum?

- Can a mission-central and culturally compatible program for adults make your institution more sustainable financially?

- Do you see partnerships with local and regional corporations as a possibility for new revenue streams and educational opportunities?

- Do you believe that packages of classes (badges, certificates etc.) designed specifically for corporations and individuals will be as relevant as degrees in the next decades?

- Does your institution have the ability to move with speed to design curriculum that the adult market is demanding?

- Would the faculty at your institution understand and embrace the learning-designer model?

- Have you explored whether alumni at your institution would be open to continuous career education as a part of their ongoing relationship with you?

Opportunity and Inclusion: Diversifying the Campus Culture

The powerful alchemy of issues of access combined with the still-profound realities around diversity and inclusion in our country today presents higher education with one of the most compelling challenges in the history of its existence: how can we reimagine our institutions as models of opportunity and inclusion, committing deeply to the notion that a transformative education should be open, available, welcoming, and supported for all? For decades, we have relied on high-stakes standardized tests that are racially, culturally, and socioeconomically biased. We structure our admissions and financial aid largely around these test scores and school-district rankings. As a result, we reinforce a culture of elitism across higher education, excluding vast populations of students for whom education is the single most critical element in their empowerment and socioeconomic mobility.

Additionally, the demographic data regarding the students that will be matriculating in the next thirty years paints a clear and compelling picture that should create urgency for leadership everywhere: the makeup of the student body of the future is changing rapidly, becoming more and more diverse across lines of race, ethnicity, religion, ability and disability, socioeconomic status, gender expression, and sexual orientation. We know that these diverse groups have been historically limited in their access to higher education, and/or not appropriately supported and served once on campus. Universities have too long been elevated by whom and how many they keep out, rather than whom they admit and graduate. Make no mistake: the new university will reallocate their measures of success from who is not admitted to the transformations of their students, and the good they do in the world after attaining their degree. The time to pivot in this direction is now.

The authors do not purport to understand all of the experiences of the rich diversity of underrepresented groups in the American experience. What we do bring is a values-based commitment to use our voices to advance the critical national causes of access, opportunity, diversity, and inclusion—and an unequivocal belief that higher education bears a deep responsibility to lead through them. We believe colleges and universities can become pioneering examples of intentional, representative communities that model a considerably more just and civil society. First, we'll examine the historical gatekeepers controlling institutional access and the limitations they place on the powerful futures those institutions support. Next, from the many necessary steps to bring change to our campuses, we'll examine some fundamental starting points: adopting a strong framework to ground ongoing efforts, constructing conversations to speak openly about bias and attitudes, and the recruitment of faculty and staff of underrepresented groups. Each of these steps is deepened by the other, and they are necessary for the richer goals that come with inclusion. Lastly, this chapter will end where we started: with the need for presidents to dedicate themselves to this cause with words, actions, and a commitment to make this work part of the embedded culture of the new university into the future.

For centuries, higher education in college and university settings was for the elite. That elite was almost exclusively male, and almost always reflected the dominant racial or ethnic group that controlled society at the time. This education also was usually controlled by the dominant religion, and faith controlled access to knowledge. This reality went largely unchallenged for centuries until the emergence of the Enlightenment and then again through the democratic age beginning with the American, French, and later European revolutions of the nineteenth century.

In the post-World War II era, educational access greatly expanded. The advent of the GI Bill and the Great Society programs under President Lyndon Johnson significantly opened the doors to people of color and others through a series of programs (e.g., Pell Grants, Perkins Loans, etc.) that expanded admissions, particularly at public institutions, and increased affordability. Over time, college enrollment among high school graduates rose from roughly 40 percent in 1960 to well over 65 percent by 2000.[51] Yet even amidst the greatest expansion of access in our history, systems of oppression, racial and ethnic biases, issues of affordability, arbitrary admission

---

51 "Immediate College Enrollment Rate," National Center for Education Statistics, last modified January 2018, https://nces.ed.gov/programs/coe/indicator_cpa. asp; "120 Years of American Education: A Statistical Portrait," National Center for Education Statistics, accessed October 15, 2018, https://nces.ed.gov/ pubs93/93442.pdf.

standards, flawed standardized testing, cultural challenges, and changing demographics have still kept many from realizing the opportunity of a college education. According to the National Student Clearinghouse, Black and Hispanic students still have a completion rate 20 percent lower than white and Asian students.[52] Addressing the issues of opportunity and inclusion that underpin our industry is one of the most significant challenges, and greatest opportunities, of the coming decade.

Elitism and Access

There remains a fundamentally embedded precept of restricting access in contemporary universities. There is an intellectual bias in certain tiers of institutions reflected in the following quote we have heard time and again: "College is not for everyone," or more insidiously, "not everyone belongs here." This form of exclusion has remained prevalent, and it is alive and thriving today. One could say it is the most omnipresent "ism" that abounds in education: elitism. This bias has helped to create a ranking system of universities based on selectivity, the logic of which goes something like this: universities are considered better if they are more difficult to get into. If they are more difficult to get into, they are more exclusive. If you can't afford it or cannot get in, then you need to focus on some other option: a "lesser" school, a shorter program or course, or entering the workforce.

Stanford University acknowledged the perils of reinforcing the notion of selectivity, vowing to stop issuing press releases about

---

52   D. Shapiro et al., "Completing College: A National View of Student Attainment Rates by Race and Ethnicity – Fall 2010 Cohort," National Student Clearinghouse Research Center, December 2016, https://nscresearchcenter.org/wp-content/uploads/SignatureReport12.pdf.

its application data. Provost Persis Drell said, "We want students to know that when we encourage them to apply to Stanford, it's not because we wish to be known as a most competitive university with a low admit rate. It is because we want promising students of all backgrounds to seriously consider the educational opportunities and possibilities at Stanford."[53] Ultimately, while a small step, a move away from a focus on selectivity can begin to allow higher education to focus on the real question at hand: If we believe intrinsically in the value of a liberal arts education in its contribution to the holistic development of individuals, why would we not want every student, no matter his or her desired path or high school academic performance, to have access to such learning?

The Myths We Tell About Testing and Admission Standards

The high-school-to-college preparation and recruitment system in its current construct limits access and success. Standardized tests, high school GPAs, letters of recommendation, admission policies, wait lists: these tools have helped to shape who is admitted to universities, but more importantly, who is not. Entire ranking mechanisms (*US News & World Report* and the *Princeton Review*, to name two) are used as tools for determining perceived quality and worth. What we know about tests after decades of study is that they are culturally and socioeconomically biased, and evidence increasingly shows that quality students are overlooked based on an overreliance on standardized testing at admissions.[54] The American Council on

53   Scott Jaschik, "Stanford Won't Boast About Applications or Admit Rates Any More," Inside Higher Ed, September 4, 2018, https://www.insidehighered.com/admissions/article/2018/09/04/stanford-will-stop-telling-world-about-its-admission-rates.

54   Richard V. Reeves and Dimitrios Halikias, "Race gaps in SAT scores highlight inequality and hinder upward mobility," Brookings

Education provides an extensive review of admissions practices in the report at this footnote.[55] An additional mitigating factor to our reliance on such testing is that they are administered to teenagers in high school in what can only be called a high-stakes environment at a time when their emotional, intellectual, and psychological maturity is in various stages of maturation.[56] Any number of internal, environmental, and economic variables can and do impact a teenager's ability to score highly on tests, from socioeconomic status to emotional development to family stability, diet, and social relationships. When we think about the flawed nature of testing, the conditions under which tests are administered, and the research findings on brain development, reliance on standardized tests to determine who is worthy of admission represents a disconnect from important research findings in education over the past thirty years: individual brains work differently, process information differently, and learn differently; therefore, teaching and measuring all the in the same manner hinders the success of those who don't learn that way.

Several generations of educators have come to rely on these less-than-ideal measures because they are easy to use and simple to categorize, despite how those measures reinforce flawed biases about students' intellectual abilities. While the tide has begun to turn away from using test scores as a central component of admissions,[57]

Institution, February 1, 2017, https://www.brookings.edu/research/race-gaps-in-sat-scores-highlight-inequality-and-hinder-upward-mobility/.:

55   Lorelle L. Espinosa, Matthew N. Gaertner, and Gary Orfield, "Race, Class, and College Access: Achieving Diversity in a Shifting Legal Landscape," American Council on Education, 2015, http://www.acenet.edu/news-room/Documents/Race-Class-and-College-Access-Achieving-Diversity-in-a-Shifting-Legal-Landscape.pdf.

56   Mariam Arain et al.,"Mutation of the Adolescent Brain,"Dove Press, National Institutes of Health, April 3, 2013, https://www.ncbi.nlm.nih.gov/pmc/articles/PMC3621648/.

57   Joseph Soares, "More Colleges Than Ever Have Test Optional Admissions Policies, and That's A Good Thing," The Conversation, January 2018, http://

educators and researchers are still divided on the value of test scores in determining a student's set of collegiate choices and trajectory. More and more new research shows, though, that a move away from testing requirements does, in fact, increase student access and institutional diversity. A significant study released in 2018 examined record-level data for nearly a million applicants at twenty-eight test-optional public and private non-profit institutions across the country and found that test-optional policies increased total numbers of applications and applications by underrepresented groups. The study also showed equivalent or higher college completion rates in students who chose not to submit test scores versus those who did.[58] A summary shared by the dot-com "Inside Higher Ed" recaps some of the most significant findings:[59]

The conclusion of the new report says the findings show that tests indeed fail to identify talented applicants who can succeed in higher education—and that applicants who opt not to submit scores are in many cases making wise decisions. The test-optional movement, they write, reflects a broader shift in society away from "a narrow assessment" of potential. Among the findings from the sample studied:

- The years following adoption of a test-optional policy saw increases in the total number of applications—by an

theconversation.com/more-colleges-than-ever-have-test-optional-admissions-policies-and-thats-a-good-thing-89852.

58 Steven T. Syverson, Valerie W. Franks, and William C. Hiss, "Defining Access: How Test Optional Works," National Association for College Admission Counseling, 2018, https://www.nacacnet.org/globalassets/documents/publications/research/defining-access-report-2018.pdf.

59 Scott Jaschik, "Making the Case for Test Optional,"Inside Higher Ed, April 27, 2018, https://www.insidehighered.com/news/2018/04/27/large-study-finds-colleges-go-test-optional-become-more-diverse-and-maintain.

average of 29 percent at private institutions and 11 percent at public institutions.

- While the degrees varied, institutions that went test-optional saw gains in the numbers of Black and Latino students applying and being admitted to their institutions.

- About one-fourth of all applicants to the test-optional colleges opted not to submit scores. (The colleges studied all consider the SAT or ACT scores of those who submit them.)

- Underrepresented minority students were more likely than others to decide not to submit. Among Black students, 35 percent opted not to submit. But the figure was only 18 percent for white students. (Women were more likely than men to decide not to submit scores.)

- "Non-submitters" (as the report termed those who didn't submit scores) were slightly less likely to be admitted to the colleges to which they applied, but their yield (the rates at which accepted applicants enroll) was higher.

- First-year grades were slightly lower for non-submitters, but they ended up highly successful, graduating at equivalent rates or, at some institutions, slightly higher rates than did those who submitted test scores. This, the report says, is "the ultimate proof of success."

The research is clear: gauging someone's future success by poor past performance against standardized test measures erects false barriers for any number of students deserving of a postsecondary education. The new university can change these barriers to access through a fundamental reboot of the admissions process. Instead, beyond certain baseline standards of admission (high school graduation), learning diagnostic tools administered during the admission process will give educators a sense of how students learn, what best methods of instruction can work, and what students need to maximize their learning. The new university will examine students as individuals to ascertain their ability to persevere and overcome challenges in their education[60], more appropriately and holistically determining their ability to be successful within the context of that particular institution and admitting them accordingly.

From Creating Opportunity to Building Inclusion

The supreme challenge of higher education today and tomorrow is not simply to achieve structural diversity: i.e., trying to achieve certain numbers of students from underrepresented groups.[61] It is to commit to the deeper and more meaningful work which involves allowing others to fully realize their potential through their identity, to think critically about social constructs in society, to respectfully engage with others in the context of work and life, and to challenge and eliminate elitism in higher education and replace it with a culture of inclusion. Universities must engage in a series of long-term measures that create this culture of inclusion for all members of the campus community. Here's where we believe these efforts start:

- Universities must introduce, adopt, and reinforce **a strong framework** to ground inclusion and equity efforts.

---

60   A. Duckworth, *Grit: The Power of Passion and Perseverance* (Toronto: Harper Collins, 2016).

61   Gary R. Pike and George D. Kuh, "Relationships among Structural Diversity, Informal Peer Interactions and Perceptions of the Campus Environment," The Review of Higher Education, 2006, http://cpr.indiana.edu/uploads/Pike%20 Kuh%20divefrsity%20RHE%202006.pdf.

- Universities must intentionally construct conversations that help students, faculty, and staff understand and **speak openly about bias and attitudes**, with a focus on bringing student groups and organizations together to **build connections, understanding, and appreciation** for diverse experiences.

- Universities must **recruit and retain** faculty and staff of underrepresented groups who can connect with and support students through the cultural and social challenges they may face, while also bringing new and important voices to institutional conversations.

- The college or university president must **act as the central champion** for diversity and inclusion.

1. Adopting a Framework to Ground Efforts

With important but disparate diversity resources spread across our campuses—from human resources to student affairs to the enrollment office to academic affairs—true culture change can only be achieved with the adoption of a framework that contextualizes, contains, and guides diversity and inclusion work at a strategic, cross-functional level. Damon A. Williams writes, "If we can give this loosely connected organizational structure a stronger conceptual tethering, we see capacities despite different administrative locations have the potential to link together in new and powerful ways, particularly at those institutions that desire to create a more rigorous, disciplined, and cohesive campus diversity agenda." Three dominant models exist that offer opportunities for institutions to enter into diversity and inclusion work as summarized by Williams in *Strategic Diversity Leadership*:

- **Level One: The Affirmative-Action and Equity Model.**
  Originating and evolving between the 1950s and the
  1970s with social justice at its core, the equity model
  aims to increase demographic diversity of the campus
  community from administration to students, eliminating
  discriminatory policies and practices. With an emphasis on
  legislative and organizational policy, this model represents
  an operational approach to the removal of institutional
  obstacles for diverse populations, while largely neglecting
  the engagement of those populations during their
  collegiate experience.

- **Level Two: The Multicultural and Inclusion-
  Diversity Model.** Beginning in the 1960s and 1970s and
  rooted in the cultural movements of those decades, the
  multicultural and inclusion model seeks to embrace
  the diverse identities and experiences of underserved
  and underrepresented groups through building mutual
  appreciation and appreciating differences. Focusing
  primarily on students and with a concentration of efforts
  along racial, ethnic, social-identity, and gender lines, this
  model led to much of the expansion of diversity services
  and units across the student-affairs division, as well as
  to a variety of new programs and institutes focused-on-
  ethnic studies, gender studies, and international studies.
  Where the multicultural and inclusion model falls short
  is in creating connections between these services and
  academic schools and critical institutional outcomes
  such as retention, moving beyond only the social-justice
  and appreciative value of multicultural engagement and
  linking it to broader educational benefits.

- **Level Three: The Learning, Diversity, and Research Model.** Emerging in the late 1990s, the learning and diversity model "recognizes, at long last, the educational and social benefits of a diverse student body, as well as the scholarly opportunities for advancing research around issues of diversity, equity, and inclusion. More than any other, this model is firmly anchored in the intellectual core of the academy," writes Williams. Driven by so many of the societal and cultural change agents we examine in this book—demographics, the needs of the workplace, growing inequality, and increasing ideological polarization—the learning and diversity model connects an individual's cognitive exploration of these complex issues to the importance of relational group dynamics and skills to the need for a deeper academic understanding of diversity. In short, when applied effectively, this model connects most clearly to diversity and inclusion as critical components of student learning and thinking.

See chapter three in Williams' book (*Higher Education Organizational Diversity Models*) for a clear, in-depth explication of the three predominant diversity models, including drivers and limitations.[62]

Universities must assess their institutional readiness for the implementation of a diversity and inclusion framework. Frequently, external assessment is useful and needed in order to truly examine the institution's environment and explicate any issues of which leadership may not be fully aware. Once that assessment is made, a strategy can be developed that draws upon the best elements of all

---

62   Damon A Williams, *Strategic Diversity Leadership* (Virginia: Stylus Publishing, 2013).

three models to move the university toward being a truly diverse and inclusive community.

2. Creating Conversations Around Bias and Inclusivity

Universities should serve as places where diverse thought can be explored, analyzed, and understood in terms of its origin and impact. Within this exploration rests a profound commitment to open, often difficult dialogue about deep-seated issues that have plagued American society for decades, if not centuries. Too often, given the inherent prejudices we fight individually and collectively every day, that dialogue is not explicated in a truly educative way that fosters understanding from a place of appreciation and awareness. A principle of context before content offers a strong position from which to launch bias and inclusivity programming. Conversations must begin with an understanding of context based on individual diverse journeys, the challenges they have faced, the history of their culture and its dynamics, and how identity shapes experience. After that is established consistently and intentionally, then issues, experiences, and perspectives can be shared, and over time, culture can shift.

We embrace a robust definition of the word "programming" in this context—not to be confused with isolated point-in-time events, we think of programming as multi-layered, iterative, continuous engagement, connected always to institutional mission and vision. Where little institutional memory exists to underpin the ongoing nature of this work, programming must be reinforced constantly in order to be effective. In order to lean in effectively to supporting open student conversations, ongoing faculty and staff programming around issues of diversity and inclusion must be developed and implemented across a wide spectrum of areas. This programming should educate existing employees about diverse workplaces, multicultural values, and opportunities and issues that arise within a diverse population, and it should help them confront their own biases. Ongoing campus employee diversity education should be combined with support and mentoring programs for new employees to effectively join the evolving inclusive campus culture. In this way, the university can intentionally bring all constituents along in reorienting the culture.

When it comes to engaging our students in bias and inclusivity conversations, the concept of "safe spaces" has pushed higher-education leaders to carefully examine the balance of our commitment to our students and to free speech. Multiple definitions of safe spaces are currently in use, confusing both those in our sector and across the media. We must clearly define the term among faculty and staff and across our campus community and take an unequivocal stand on the role of higher education as it relates to encouraging open debate. Four definitions are most common:

1. The creation of a safe space can be defined as **the ability of a group of individuals with a similar identity, background, or set of experiences to gather together in order to explore that identity, background, or experience with openness, and without fear of attack or ridicule.** A multicultural group, an LGBTQI club, and a sexual-assault-victims' organization are examples of a healthy articulation of safe spaces. All students deserve to feel fundamentally safe on our campuses. These communities, most frequently formed around particularly vulnerable or underrepresented populations, can offer a level of emotional protection that can be critical to their

well-being and ability to engage successfully in their learning.

2. The phrase safe space is also used to describe **an academic environment in which all individuals are encouraged to "speak, take intellectual risks, and explore any line of thought."** In this context, safety is focused on the ability and right of the speaker to engage in free speech and critical thinking around the topic at hand. In this scenario on most of our campuses, those in the conversation will represent different perspectives and experiences, and should all be allowed to bring rational, fact-based argument to the table without fear that he or she will, for example, be graded poorly because of an opinion that differs from that of the professor. Academic protection is deeply aligned with an individual's first-amendment rights and ensures an academy that welcomes and encourages freedom of thought as critical to intellectual development.

3. Safe space can also be defined **as people's reasonable expectation to not have to defend or debate their beliefs in the confines of their private living space.** Ashutosh Bhagwat and John Inazu wrote, "We suspect that even the most vigorous academic proponents of open debate would not want their living rooms to become open forums for diverse-viewpoint expression. Most people need to be able to retreat and rejuvenate in their homes and other intimate social settings. In these environments, people commune with like-minded friends, engage in informal interactions, and pursue mindless pastimes with

no ideological content at all … In these settings, people often do not want to have to defend their deepest beliefs, or to confront hostility. These behaviors are perfectly normal for most of us, and that includes college students."[63] Residential campuses present a uniquely challenging environment within which we must recognize that unlike faculty, staff, and administrators, residential students do not always have the option to retreat from campus for privacy.

While all three of the above safe spaces have a place in higher education, it is the fourth and newest interpretation of "safe space" that challenges the core of our work as educators. The *Harvard Political Review* article "Tackling the Term: What is a Safe Space?" examines a conflation causing consternation and inflaming passionate debate across the academy. A new iteration of the concept has emerged—some students advocate to expand emotional safe spaces to encompass the campus as a whole. This new space is a false extrapolation of the originals, mistakenly operating under the unshakable credo that in an academic setting, people should feel emotionally secure.

A problem arises in this case. There exists a tension between emotional safety and academic safety. If the goal of an academic setting is to keep people comfortable, then the acceptability of speech will be determined by how objectionable it is. And if arguments are limited based on how offensive they seem, people are expected to adhere to an implicit set of polite ideological norms. Speech is allowed so long as it doesn't appear to conflict with the socially

---

63 Ashutosh Bhagwat and John Inazu, "Searching for Safe Spaces" Inside Higher Ed, March 21, 2017, https://www.insidehighered.com/views/2017/03/21/easily-caricatured-safe-spaces-can-help-students-learn-essay.

accepted opinions on certain touchy topics. In this way, new safe spaces become less about respecting and empowering *individuals* than sanctifying certain *ideas*. Provocative speech is censored, which has pernicious effects on the academic tradition.[64]

This fourth conception of safe spaces must not be embraced by the new university. It is antithetical to intellectual exploration and does not prepare students for a world where the marketplace of ideas and perspectives is rich, varied, and often necessarily challenging.

We live in an era of heightened rhetoric with little room for thoughtful and respectful debate. As our country experiences a continued ideological polarization (i.e., choose your group and hunker down on your side), we also have tended to move away from inclusive dialogue. If society increasingly refuses to engage in civil discourse and debate, then universities must be models for how dialogue and discussion among people with widely disparate views and experiences are carried forth with respect and dignity. It is hard and powerful work that demands a high level of self-awareness and respect for those who disagree, and it means exposure to concerns and ideas that many will find difficult. But being uncomfortable is not a reason to inhibit free speech or the civil debate of issues. It is the educated and mature person who can explore, analyze, and debate viewpoints with reasoned respect and factual context. Ultimately, everyone is entitled to their own opinions, but not their own facts. That is where the debate can begin, with ensuing discussions focused on developing understanding and awareness. Modeling that kind of discourse may indeed be the most important

---

64　Katherine Ho, "Tackling the Term: What is a Safe Space?" Harvard Political Review, January 30, 2017, http://harvardpolitics.com/harvard/what-is-a-safe-space/.

lesson the university and its community members can provide to our students.

3. Recruiting Faculty and Staff with Diversity and Inclusion in Mind

Every open position provides an opportunity for a college or university to enrich the critical campus-wide discourse explored above by bringing new and different voices into the campus community. In the new university, a proactive, inclusive recruitment culture will replace a reactive, insular hiring culture. When risk-taking, innovation, and a commitment to diversity and inclusion are central, hiring must involve intentional recruitment strategies designed to develop a representative pool of candidates. Search committees must be appropriately trained and diverse in membership, no longer the sole responsibility of individual departments and schools. Specialists in a given academic or operational area can evaluate credentials and assess skill sets, and their expertise must be utilized. But a healthy recruitment culture also includes those from across campus who understand that in order to educate a diverse population, one must have a diverse and representative faculty and staff.

Four key steps are critical to reordering the search process and committee composition around a recruitment culture:

- First, search committees for each position are intentionally formed from across the campus to ensure diverse representation.

- Second, these committees explore their own biases under the direction of a Title IX coordinator and human resources director before any applicant files are reviewed.

These sessions allow the search committee to explicate their own biases regarding credentials, education, and experience, as well as tease out any biases related to underrepresented groups.

- Third, candidates of diverse backgrounds are recruited with an active approach. Job ads are placed in publications and with organizations that connect to underrepresented groups, and then candidates are actively contacted/recruited to gauge their interest.

- Fourth, file review begins only when the pool of candidates is representatively diverse. If the pool is not sufficiently representative, the pool is refreshed with additional recruitment, and if then no diversity is achieved, the search is evaluated by the president or relevant vice president to determine whether it should still go forward or be suspended and retooled.

All of these steps are followed before the broader search committee is given access to the pool for review and further steps.

4. Leading Through Diversity and Inclusion

The work here is ongoing, difficult, and eye-opening, and it takes leadership, patience, discipline, engagement, and self-awareness from all constituents: students, staff, faculty, the administration, and the board of trustees. But the central champion for diversity and access on any campus must be the president. Even an excellent chief diversity officer cannot drive institutional culture without the president's passion, time, and focus. If there is not direct leadership and responsibility for fostering diversity and inclusion, there will not be sustained efforts and clear results. The leadership dimension regarding diversity translates into a deep, on-ground commitment. Leaders who focus on diversity and inclusion stay true to several key considerations:

- They show up in the space on a consistent basis. Presidents must not announce a commitment to diversity then not show up where the dialogue is happening.

- They harbor a deep belief that these issues matter and communicate this belief consistently to all audiences.

- They understand that these issues are evolving and complex, and require thoughtful, ongoing discussion, analysis, and continual learning.

- They ensure that their administration is acting proactively to shape the campus conversation and experience of underrepresented students, not reactively managing challenges.

In short, presidents show up, communicate the value of diversity constantly, commit to personal openness and continued learning, and drive the organization to responsible action.

Leaning into issues of opportunity and inclusion is not an add-on to a university's mission, it is an imperative role of the new university. There are learners across disparate backgrounds who are deeply deserving of the types of transformative learning opportunities higher education can offer. As a consequence of lack of access, the talents and abilities of millions have been closed out of the system and denied their ability to flourish and contribute. Today, higher education has both the tools and the obligation to right that wrong, enhancing and ensuring a more diverse and inclusive university community. Colleges and universities can be the vehicle through which a vast resource of creative and intellectual energy is unleashed. It will take deep, consistent, and intentional commitment across the entire spectrum of strategy, operations, and learning, with leaders at the center of that commitment. In other words, the new university requires courageous leadership.

Opportunity and Inclusion: Diversifying the Campus Culture Challenge Questions

- Do you moderate access to your institution using standardized test scores?

- Do you have processes in place that support a recruitment and retention culture?

- Is the university as a whole moving toward a more representatively diverse campus community that is reflective of national demographic trends?

- Does your institution have cultural barriers to diversity and inclusion?

- Does the president own and lead diversity and inclusion at the highest level?

- Have you moved your institution from a passive hiring culture to a recruitment and retention culture?

- Are there campus dialogues around diversity and inclusion held on a regular basis?

- Do all of your faculty and staff engage in ongoing training/workshops on diversity and inclusion?

- Do you actively recruit and retain underrepresented groups into your senior leadership team?

- Do you promote free debate and discussion within a framework of civil discourse and respect?

- Do you create opportunities and experiences where students, faculty, and staff of diverse backgrounds and experiences can engage in conversations that enhance understanding and awareness?

Positioning to Pivot

The world is changing at an almost unfathomable pace, and we must change with it. We bear responsibility for ensuring that students of all ages have access to the tools they need in order to find their own success in that world, empowering them to make significant contributions to their communities and beyond. Developments in research, technology, and learning happen so frequently that even during our writing, we have stopped several times to tell each other that something new on the horizon needed to be examined. It is safe to say that before the ink dries on this book, there will be more for us to consider. But though the full picture of all this change may never be perfectly clear, in order to remain relevant into the future, each institution must find its own pivot and move decisively toward it. And we have an ideal environment in which to do so: colleges and universities are places where generations of people work, live, and learn side by side. This wonderful reality creates an opportunity for experimentation to be rich, nuanced, and centered around the needs of students, where ideation can be unfettered and open. In the new university, there will be not just openness, but an encouraging welcome to ideas that challenge the status quo, no matter their origin. Merit will be placed on one's ideas and the ability to implement them effectively, and the most innovative, impactful approaches to learning and research in the service of student learning will hold sway.

Inherent in a pivot at any institution is an extraordinary amount of change. At a recent presentation of new teaching technologies and methods, a faculty member observed the new methods and approaches to incorporating technology into the classroom and lamented, "I didn't sign on for this twenty years ago." Think about that statement in the context of the monumental changes in technology and research on learning that have occurred over the past two decades. This professional is fearful of the evolution of his profession because it means changing how he does his work. There is a normal fear of change embedded in that statement that we all feel at various times of our lives as new approaches emerge and take hold in our career, but there is also an element of absurdity as well—if you went to a cardiologist because you had a heart problem that needed surgery and your surgeon said, "I perform heart surgery with the same tools and knowledge and techniques that I learned twenty or thirty years before, because that's how I prefer to work," patients would leave as fast as their feet could carry them, never to return.

The world of rapid adaptation and continuous learning into which our students are entering demands our own adaptation and learning. But we do want to acknowledge the fear of change and the different ways in which people handle it. There has been a great deal of study and research done on the ability to adapt early to change and how small the percentage of the population is that will embrace it. Rogers' Technology Adoption Curve gives us an example of the challenges we intuit in our experiences with introducing new ideas, tools, and processes at our institutions:

- A mere 2.5 percent of the population are true innovators—those who have both the willingness to take risks and desire to experiment.

- Another 13.5 percent are considered early adopters—people who are more selective about what they try but are willing to step in relatively early. Others looks to the early adopters for their feedback and experience.

- A full 68 percent represent the aptly named majority, split evenly between the early majority—who adopt new ideas once they understand how it will fit into or affect their lives, and the late majority—who adopt because of peer pressure or economic necessity.

- The final 16 percent—as much of the population as the innovators and early adopters together—make decisions based on past experiences and/or are unable, economically or otherwise, to adopt new ideas.

The primary difference between these categories is an "individual's psychological disposition to new ideas"—something over which we have no influence.[65] What we can connect to, however, is the small but mighty group of innovators and early adopters who others will watch, engaging them visibly as leaders in pilot initiatives. Beginning with the willing and linking their innovative initiatives with clear outcomes has been the method used in every one of the institutions featured in this book. Sweeping change happens after small seeds of change have been nurtured for growth.

---

65 E. Rogers, *Diffusion of Innovations*, (New York: Free Press, 2003).

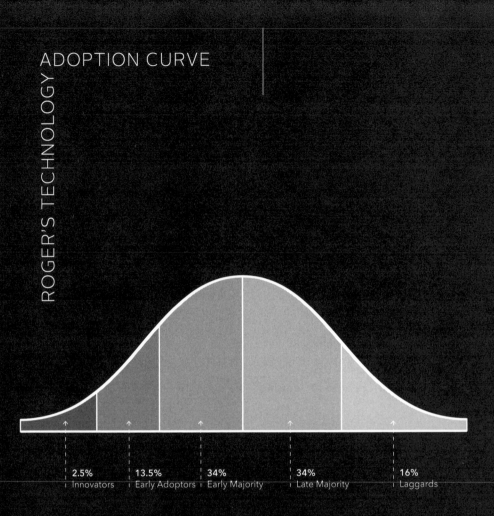

ROGER'S TECHNOLOGY

ADOPTION CURVE

| 2.5% | 13.5% | 34% | 34% | 16% |
| Innovators | Early Adoptors | Early Majority | Late Majority | Laggards |

The primary difference between these categories is an "individual's psychological disposition to new ideas" - something over which we have no influence. What we can connect to, however, is the small but mighty group of innovators and early adopters who others will watch, engaging them visibly as leaders in pilot initiatives.

Common Characteristics of Pivoting Institutions

We chose the four institutions represented here, because with all their differences, we hoped it would be possible for independent colleges and universities across the country to see themselves somewhere in these examples. DWU, Marian, Maryville, and Spelman have all experienced fragile periods at some point in their history. If this disparate group of institutions can pivot, then any college can. Although they are different in many ways, some thematic similarities point us to a critical understanding of what it takes to pivot, regardless of the institutional context.

A Visionary Culture

A trait found on every one of these campuses is a visionary culture developed by the leadership of the president and the board of trustees. The presidents of these institutions have created an atmosphere of great hope and high expectations. Innovative projects and pilot initiatives at each institution were undertaken to prove the point of determination to succeed. Now the culture of innovation and growth has been embraced at all levels, and institutional self-esteem and momentum at each campus are thriving. The people who work at these colleges believe in what they do and believe that they do it well. They are not afraid to dream and tackle difficult challenges. It is more important to them to try, even if failing at junctures along the way, than not to have tried at all. At each of these institutions there is a prevalent theme that can be stated as simply as, "We can do this!" Such courage has allowed them to move forward with agility and speed. They positioned themselves to pivot, acted quickly and decisively, and are still acting on one initiative after another with a focus on the future.

A Strategic Plan that Connects to the Vision

Each institution has a clear, actionable strategic plan that lives out its vision. The plan is understood and embraced by the campus community and the board of trustees. There is a culture of accountability for achieving the plan, and the strategic financial investments needed to make critical initiatives happen are a top priority. The planning process itself has been collaborative but with the right balance between decision-making and inclusivity. Priorities are clear, and though initiatives are highly specific, the ability to shift and seize new opportunities and innovate along the way is woven into an iterative, continuous-planning model. These strategic plans are not incremental fixes—they represent aspirational leaps to the future. Planning has taken these colleges and universities to a place where they are focused squarely on transformative student learning and innovative experiences.

An Engaged Board

At the four institutions discussed, board members have been chosen carefully for their ability to sup-port new ways of thinking academically, administratively, and with the changing needs of the work-place in mind. From their ability to embrace new learning theories to the discerning process of careful presidential selection, they have been courageous. They enjoy a rich collaboration with institutional leadership that has made them all feel that they are making a substantial and significant difference in the lives of students. If you are a board member reading this book, we challenge you to make the board at your institution as effective and innovative as possible in order to help lead a pivot. Profound board engagement is a critical component to pivoting at each of these institutions. Board members are educated about the issues of learning today and are energized, not frightened, by the innovations of tomorrow. Board members deserve to share in the hope and excitement for the future possibilities for their institutions and for higher education as a whole.

A Unified Leadership Team

Each institution we have studied has a leadership team or president's cabinet that is effective, action-oriented, and passionate. They are able to execute quickly as individuals and also function smoothly as a group. These teams listen carefully to shared discussions on vision and determine how to turn that vision into action. There is no possibility to position for a pivot without a strong, cohesive leadership team in place. When a leadership team is not functioning at the highest levels, there is an inability to activate solutions and inspire others to action. The best leadership teams also understand that they need to continue their own learning. Each of these teams you have read about have reached out for external help when it has been crucial to their success, embracing the right partners without hesitation. They have each other's backs and play in each other's sandboxes without threat and intimidation. They are healthy, functional, and engaged at all points along the way.

An Unwavering Dedication to Students

The dedication to student-centered learning inside and outside of the classroom lives at the very heart of each of these institutions. First and foremost, the leadership, faculty, and staff of these institutions nurture a deep loyalty to their students. For these colleges and universities, daily institutional life revolves around the needs of the student, with efficient operational functions creating time and space for development, learning, and creativity in service of providing learners with a rich student experience in all aspects of college life. They continue to search for ways to be sure that learning is translating into lifelong success. Advising and mentoring are present at best-practice levels, and there is a seriousness of purpose around student success at all phases of the journey.

Courage

Each institution found the courage to ask the tough questions, challenge traditional notions of higher education, explore possibilities from a variety of sources both in and outside of the sector, and to try new ideas and risk failure for the greater good of their students. Each college or university, in its own way, found the courage to recognize the changing dynamics of our world and embrace alternative ways of meeting student needs. Each continues to model for its students the courage to question, experiment, and take risks.

The circumstances of our country, our culture, our economy, and our educational system demand that all of us in higher education find ways to pivot into the future. It will take a great deal of courage and an unshakable belief that every student deserves to learn in a way that prepares him or her for life's journey. We challenge you to use this book to study in teams—leadership, board of trustees, faculty, and staff—across your institution. Innovation can start with asking the simple question: why? And end with the stimulating: what if? We hope you will find space for these conversations and weave them into your planning for the future. We urge you to position yourself to pivot, then *move*. Be an early adaptor and move ahead of the pack. We challenge you to serve your students better by committing yourselves with hope to the what if. The greatest reward for all of us will be in how those students are transformed by their experiences at our institutions, and in the world they will build from what they learn.

Appendix I: Institutional Profiles

At the time of publication, each of the four institutions featured in this book have experienced significant growth and recognition. Below you'll find a summary of institutional mission, vision, metrics, highlights, and accolades.

Dakota Wesleyan University

Strategic Vision: Dakota Wesleyan University will be recognized as a national model of higher education's innovation and impact on rural America.

Mission: As an inclusive educational community, Dakota Wesleyan University provides a transformative learning experience that cultivates enduring intellectual growth, ethically grounded leadership, intentional faith exploration, and meaningful service.

Institutional Overview:
- Located in Mitchell, South Dakota

- Senator George McGovern is the most famous alumni. The McGovern Center for Leadership and Service and the Kelley Center for Entrepreneurship offers applied and experiential learning opportunities across the curriculum.

- 44 percent first generation and 45 percent low income (2018 projections)

- 77 percent graduation rate of students in the TRiO program designed to support first-generation, low income, and disabled students (2017)

- 50 percent increase in service learning/community-based learning since 2013

- 24 percent increase in traditional, undergraduate enrollment since 2014

- 15 percent increase in retention in the past decade

- 250 percent increase in online learners since 2013

- Ten years of record enrollment growth

- Doubled institutional net assets in seven years from $31 million to $62 million

- 96 percent of staff and faculty financially give back to the university

- Digital DWU collaboration with Apple to support a 1 to 1 initiative expanding access for students of all learning backgrounds and educating faculty to equip them for digital literacy across the curriculum

- Champions of Character Gold Star Institution with the NAIA

- Core curriculum includes courses in innovation, problem-solving and creativity as well as applied leadership and a capstone project and presentation

- Over $40 million-dollar campaign completed in three and a half years—ahead of schedule and above target

- Four major building projects since 2013: 50,000-square-foot health sciences center; 90,000-square foot sport and wellness complex; 20,000-square-foot performing arts space; 30,000-square-foot residence hall; major renovations to the current wellness center, dining area, admissions, and development offices, nearly all paid through donor contributions

- Major community partnerships to support program development, scholarships, and adult learning

- Unique responsive market programs: non-profit church leadership; trust management; digital media and design; LPN-BS in nursing.

- Selected as "Great Place to Work" by *Prairie Business Magazine* (one of forty selected out of thirteen hundred nominees and the only university on the list)

- Significant partnerships across the region to support labor-force development

- Articulation agreements with regional technical institutes and community colleges

- For the last nine years, the university has run a budget in the black. New, targeted online programs designed to meet regional labor-force demands have grown by more than

250 percent in three years, meeting both the institution's mission and need for increasing and diversified revenue streams

Marian University

Vision: At Marian University, our vision is to provide an education distinguished in its ability to prepare transformative leaders for service to the world.

Mission: Our mission is to be a great Catholic university dedicated to providing students with excellent teaching and learning in the Franciscan and liberal arts tradition. We welcome students of all faiths who seek an educational experience framed within the context of our Franciscan values of dignity of the individual, peace and justice, reconciliation, and responsible stewardship. Our understanding of these values is informed by reflection on the life of Jesus Christ and prayer.

Institutional Overview:

- Located in Indianapolis, Indiana
- Affiliated with the Sisters of St. Francis, Oldenburg, Indiana
- 80 percent FTFT Retention (up from 59 percent in 2001)
- $36 million endowment
- $129.1 million in net assets (up from $8.9 million in 2001)
- $111.1 million annual revenue (up from $14.1 million in 2001)

- $2 million per month average in fundraising (up from $1.5 million for the year in 2001)

- Just over $40 million in new construction completed between 2016 and 2018

- Over four thousand total students in 2018–19 academic year (up from 1,100 students in 2001)

- 1,126 graduate students (up from twelve in 2001), with more than six hundred in the college of osteopathic medicine

- Forty-two undergraduate programs

- Eleven master's degree programs

- Three doctoral programs

- 36.2 percent Pell-eligible

- 17.5 percent first-generation students

- Fourth-fastest growing Catholic baccalaureate college in the country[66]

- 99 percent of full-time enrolled freshmen receive scholarships and grants

- Forty-five states and twenty-three nations are represented in the student population

- 13:1 student-faculty ratio

- MU athletics has won thirty-eight USA Cycling National Championships

- The two hundred-acre campus includes the fifty-five-acre wetland and lowland forest known as the Nina Mason

---

66   According to the 2016 Almanac published by the Chronicle for Higher Ed.

Pulliam EcoLab and the Indy Cycloplex, home to the Major Taylor Velodrome, hosting races, clinics, and other cycling events

Maryville University

Strategic Vision: Maryville will be the innovative leader in higher education promoting a revolution in student learning that expands access and opportunities for all.

Mission: Maryville University is an outstanding national university offering a comprehensive and innovative education focused on student learning, outcomes, and success. This education is built upon an innovative liberal arts foundation leading to compelling programs in the arts and sciences, health professions, education, and business that prepare students for a life of engagement and achievement in multiple fields of endeavor.

Institutional Overview:

- Located twenty miles west of downtown St. Louis, Missouri

- Historically affiliated with the Sisters of the Sacred Heart

- 9,300 students: 3,600 undergraduate (traditional and adult) students, 5,700 graduate students (960 on-campus, 4,700 online)

- Retention Rate: 88 percent

- Student-faculty ratio: 14:1

- 97 percent job-placement rate

- Four-year graduation rate: 72 percent

- 93 percent of full-time students receive aid

- $53 million in aid distributed last year

- Offering over ninety degree programs: twenty-five online degrees, nineteen masters programs, five doctoral programs

- 275 international students

- Third fastest-growing private university in the nation, according to *Chronicle of Higher Education*

- Five nationally ranked programs: nursing, cybersecurity, sports business management, interior design, actuarial science

- Named an Apple Distinguished School for 2016–2018; recognized for its Digital World program, which gives students the opportunity to personalize their education in an enhanced technology environment

- Ranked in the top 10 percent of all major universities in the nation for the economic value of its academic degrees by Educate to Career, a non-profit firm that analyzes the value of a college degree in response to student demand for good return on investment (ROI)

- Consistently ranked by *Forbes* and Kiplinger's Personal Finance magazines as a top private school; named by *Kiplinger's* to its list of one hundred best values in private colleges and universities for seven consecutive years; named by *Forbes* to its "Best Colleges" list for the past three years

Spelman College

Strategic Vision: Grounded in our compelling mission and value propositions, we will propel Spelman College into the top tier of liberal arts institutions.

Mission: Spelman College, a historically Black college and a global leader in the education of women of African descent, is dedicated to academic excellence in the liberal arts and sciences and the intellectual, creative, ethical, and leadership development of its students. Spelman empowers the whole person to engage the many cultures of the world and inspires a commitment to positive social change.

Institutional Overview:

- Fourth historically Black female institution of higher education to receive its collegiate charter and oldest private historically Black liberal arts college for women

- A member of the Atlanta University Center academic consortium

- 2,100 students

- Forty-one states and fifteen nations represented

- 76 percent graduation rate, the highest rate among HBCUs

- Acceptance rate of 41 percent, among the most selective women's colleges in the nation

- 89 percent of students receive financial aid

- 42 percent of average need met

- 48 percent of students are PELL eligible

- 10:1 student-faculty ratio

- 1:4 ratio of computers available for student use

- Most popular majors are biological and biomedical sciences, English, physical therapy, psychology, and social sciences

- Two-thirds of graduates go on to obtain advanced degrees

- Eighty-two student organizations including community service organizations, choral and music ensembles, jazz band, intramural sports, and Morehouse cheerleading squad

- Annual budget of over $112 million

- Recognized as one of the leading producers of Fulbright Fellowship winners

- 88 percent of faculty members have the highest degrees in their fields

- Recognized by the National Science Foundation as the leading producer of Black women who go on to earn doctorate degrees in the sciences

- Ranked number one HBCU by the U.S. News & World Report

- Ranked number two in Best Value Schools—Best Historically Black Colleges and Institutions

- Ranked number three for Students' Top Schools for Inspiration by the *Wall Street Journal*/Times Higher Education Survey

- Ranked among the top fifty colleges in the south by *Money* magazine

- Ranked among the top twenty best women's colleges by BestColleges.com

- Listed among College Magazine's top ten schools for activists

- Listed among Peace Corps' 2016 top volunteer-producing Historically Black Colleges and Universities

- The Spelman College Museum of Fine Art is the only museum in the country to focus on collections by and about women of the African Diaspora

- In 2013, Spelman dropped varsity athletics, and used those budgeted funds to create a wellness program open to all students

- Notable Alumnae include: Alice Walker, Marian Wright Edelman, Keshia Knight Pulliam, Esther Rolle, Rolonda Watts, Leslie Sykes, Maia Campbell, Bernice Johnson Reagon, and Janet Bragg

Appendix II: Author Biographies

Joanne Soliday

Joanne Soliday is a higher education consultant and strategic planning specialist with over thirty years of experience on college and university campuses. Following leadership positions on two college campuses, Joanne became a founding partner of Credo, a consulting firm focused on independent higher education. Since 2001, Joanne has had the privilege of working with more than two hundred and fifty private colleges and universities. Her work with these institutions inspired her to author *Surviving to Thriving: A Planning Framework for Leaders of Private Colleges and Universities*. Now in its second edition, her book is being used nationally to assist college leadership teams in planning for their futures.

After earning her bachelor's degree in education from West Virginia Wesleyan College, Joanne taught in the Connecticut and North Carolina public school systems before becoming director of consultation and education at Alamance County Mental Health

Center. She transitioned to higher education, joining the staff at Elon University, where she remained for eighteen years. She was part of an administrative team that helped transformed Elon into one of the nation's most nationally acclaimed universities. While there, she held a number of key positions including director of special projects, associate dean of students affairs, director of external relations, director of the Elon Society, and dean of admissions and financial planning. Upon leaving Elon, Joanne returned to her alma mater to serve as vice president for advancement and enrollment.

Since her retirement from full-time consulting in 2014, Joanne has served as a presenter and keynote speaker at higher-education conferences across the country and is privileged to be engaged in many formal coaching relationships as a strategic advisor to independent college presidents. In 2016, Joanne was awarded an honorary doctorate of humane letters by her alma mater.

In addition to her undergraduate degree from West Virginia Wesleyan College, she also earned a MEd from the University of North Carolina at Chapel Hill and has pursued divinity studies at Duke University. Joanne is an ordained minister and serves as a pastor and elder at St. Mark's Church in Burlington, North Carolina. She is married to Keith Soliday and has three children and four grandchildren.

Dr. Mark Lombardi

Dr. Mark Lombardi is the tenth president of Maryville University and has served there since 2007. During his tenure, Maryville University has tripled enrollment to more than ninety-three hundred students hailing from fifty states and sixty countries. In 2017, the *Chronicle of Higher Education* recognized Maryville as the third fastest-growing private university in the nation, and in 2013 and 2014 *US News & World*

Report recognized Maryville as the number-one overperforming university in the country. Maryville received the Apple Distinguished School designation for 2016–2018 for innovation, leadership, educational excellence and a clear vision of exemplary learning environments. In addition, Maryville has also been ranked in the top 15 percent of universities nationwide for ROI for three consecutive years.

For over twenty-five years, at three different institutions, Dr. Lombardi has served as a tenured faculty member in political science and international relations, department chair, director of international programs, vice president for academic affairs, provost and president. Dr. Lombardi also served as executive director of the US-Africa Education Foundation.

In addition to fundraising initiatives that have netted over $125 million for projects in the arts, academic learning space, international programs, learning technology and student services, Dr. Lombardi has appeared in more than two hundred interviews for radio and television on politics, international issues, and innovation and the future of higher education. He is a noted author, publishing several articles and three books, one of which is now in its tenth edition. Dr. Lombardi earned a PhD and master's degree in political science and international relations from The Ohio State University and a bachelor's degree in political science from Purdue University.